hugo

Portuguese
in Three Months

Maria Fernanda Allen

A Dorling Kindersley Book
www.dk.com

A DORLING KINDERSLEY BOOK

www.dk.com

This new and enlarged edition published in Great Britain
in 1997 by Hugo's Language Books,
an imprint of Dorling Kindersley Limited,
9 Henrietta Street, London WC2E 8PS

A CIP catalogue record is available from the British Library.

ISBN 0 85285 303 3

Portuguese in Three Months is also available in
a pack with four cassettes, ISBN 0 85285 304 1

Written by

Maria Fernanda Allen
Lecturer in Portuguese at the University of Westminster
(Post-Graduate Dept. and other courses) and a
Fellow of the Institute of Linguists

Set in 10/12pt Palatino by
Andrew Burrell
Printed and bound by LegoPrint, Italy

Preface

This new edition of 'Portuguese in Three Months' has been written for us by Maria Fernanda Allen, whose experience in teaching her native tongue ranges from beginners to post-graduate level. She has drawn on this expertise to produce a simple yet complete course for students aiming to acquire a good working knowledge of the language in a short time and who will probably be studying alone at home.

The book begins with an explanation of Portuguese pronunciation as far as this is possible without going too deeply into all the nuances and varying sounds involved. If you are working without a teacher, you should find that our system of 'imitated pronunciation' simplifies matters considerably. Using the book together with our cassette recordings (allowing you to hear the Portuguese text at the same time that you read it) is an ideal combination, giving another dimension to the course.

It has always been a principle of the Hugo method to teach only what is really essential. We assume that the student wants to learn Portuguese from a practical angle; the chapters contain those rules of grammar that will be of most use in this respect. Constructions are clearly explained, and the order in which everything is presented takes into consideration the need for rapid progress. Each chapter includes exercises and conversation drills; later in the course you will move on to the use of idiom and colloquialisms, so necessary for a thorough grasp of conversational Portuguese. Further help with reading and comprehension, in the form of extracts from modern authors and letter-writing styles, plus a selection of useful sentences and words arranged in phrasebook fashion and designed to widen your vocabulary, round off the course. An appendix lists verb formations and irregularities.

Ideally you should spend about an hour a day on your work (slightly less, maybe, if you do not use the cassette recordings), although there is no hard and fast rule on this. Do as much as you feel capable of doing; if you have no special aptitude for language-learning, there is no point in forcing yourself beyond your daily capacity to assimilate new material. It is much better to learn a little at a time, and to learn that thoroughly. .

In studying the chapters, first read each rule or numbered section carefully and re-read it to ensure that you have fully understood the grammar, then translate the following exercise(s) by writing down the answers. Check these by referring to the key at the back of the book; if you have made too many mistakes, go back over the instruction before attempting the same questions again. Every now and then, you'll find a *Practice!* section which gives you more vocabulary and exercises. The conversational exercises should be read aloud and their constructions carefully noted. If you have the cassette recordings, you should listen to these at the same time as you read the instruction and the examples. See how closely you can imitate the voices on the recording.

When you think you have completed a section satisfactorily (alternatively, just before your daily study period is over) go back over what you have recently done, to ensure that it is firmly committed to memory. Once you are through the first few chapters and have a good grasp of elementary grammar, dip into the idioms and reading passages, thereby increasing your vocabulary and your comprehension of both written and spoken Portuguese. When the course is completed, you should have a very good understanding of the language - more than sufficient for general holiday or business purposes, and enough to lead quickly into an examination syllabus if this is your eventual aim.

Contents

6

Pronunciation

In order to understand phonetics, and in particular our system of imitated pronunciation, it is essential to learn a few rules about syllables. These are groups of two or three letters which must include a vowel representing one sound.

A Portuguese word is automatically stressed on the last but one syllable (no accent mark is required) unless the word has an accent mark elsewhere or ends in an oral diphthong (see page 10), an **l**, **r**, **z** or **i** (provided the **i** isn't part of the diphthong). For example, **marmelada** has four syllables (mar me *la* da) and according to the rule it is stressed on the penultimate *(la)*. As a result of this, the sound of the stressed *a* becomes open [ah] while the other a's remain mute [er].

Accent marks you will see in Portuguese are: the acute (´), the grave (`), the tilde (~) and the circumflex (^).

The Imitated Pronunciation

Given the complex sound structure of Portuguese it is not always possible to transcribe its pronunciation in terms of English spelling. Nonetheless, the following notes should enable you to master with ease the most elusive as well as the most obvious Portuguese sounds. Of much greater help. naturally, would be the cassette recordings which Hugo's have produced: these allow you to hear the Portuguese words and phrases at the same time as you read them in the book. When studying this on your own, without a Portuguese teacher to talk to, then the complete Cassette Course makes everything much easier.

When reading the imitated pronunciation, avoid pauses between the syllables. Pronounce these as if they formed part of an English word, emphasising the one printed with a stress mark (') before it. The Portuguese have an irrepressible tendency to link the sound of a terminal vowel with the beginning of the next word; this liaison results in **ele era** sounding like el-'leh-re, or **nove horas** ('noh've and 'oh-rersh) becoming noh-'voh-rersh.

The Portuguese alphabet

A	B	C	D	E	F	G	H
[ah]	[bay]	[say]	[day]	[eh]	[eff]	[zhay*]	['er-gah]

I	J	L	M	N	O	P	Q
[ee]	['zhoh-ter]	[ell]	[emm]	[enn]	[oh]	[pay]	[kay]

R	S	T	U	V	X	Z
[err]	[ess]	[tay]	[oo]	[vay]	[sheesh]	[zay]

The letters K ['kah-per], W ['doo-ble vay] and Y [ee-'gray-goo] are not in use today, except when they refer to foreign names, chemistry symbols and so on.

* The G and J are pronounced like s in the English word 'measure'; this sound is represented by zh in our imitated pronunciation. When G has a hard sound (consult the imitated pronunciation guide that follows) it will be represented by g, as in 'girl'.

Whenever you see a letter r in italics (as in 'zhoh-ter, 'er-gah), usually after an e in the imitated syllables, remember that it is **not to be pronounced.** It is there in order to ensure that you give the correct sound: without this r you might turn 'zhoh-ter into 'zhoh-te - and make too much of the ending so that it became -tee, which would be quite wrong. Equally wrong would be -ter.

Vowels

a
This is open (as in 'father') in a stressed syllable, before l or final **r**, and when it has an acute or grave accent. Otherwise it is mute, like the u in 'but'.
camada [ker-'mah-der] layer
falar [fer-'lahr] to speak
animal [er-nee-'mahl] animal
chá [shah] tea

Becomes nasal when under a tilde mark (ã); the italic n we use to indicate this sound should not be pronounced as a proper n, but more like the end of 'lung' without making much of the g. For example: **irmã** ['eer-ma*n*] sister
When it is under a circumflex the a remains mute, but this syllable, which is usually the third from the end, will be stressed instead of the usual last but one syllable:
alfândega [al-fa*n*-de-ger] Customs

e
Has an open sound (as in 'vet') in a stressed syllable, before l and under grave or acute accents. Unstressed, it is mute (as e in 'mute'). In Brazil, this mute sound is replaced by ee.
metro ['meh-troo] metre, underground (railway)
café [ker-'feh] coffee
mel [mehl] honey
secretária (se-kre-'tah-ree-er) secretary

The 'close **e**', pronounced similarly to the first e in 'seance', occurs in some stressed syllables, under a circumflex accent and before a final **r**.
pelo ['pay-loo] of the, by the
comer [koo-'mayr] to eat
vê [vay] see

When an **e** is by itself or forms the first syllable on its own it is pronounced as the English e in 'see'.
edifício [ee-dee-'fee-sy'oo] edifice, building

i
This is always pronounced 'ee', but when unstressed it should be given a shorter (close) sound.
parti [per-'tee] I left

o
In a stressed position, or if it has an acute accent or comes before **l**, the sound of **o** is open (similar to a in 'fall').
avó [er-'voh] grandmother
sol [sohl] sun
morte ['mohr'te] death

It has a close sound similar to o in 'mole' in some stressed syllables, before final **r**, and with the circumflex accent. This is the most used sound in Brazil, with oo being heard at the end of a word.
avô [er-'voh] grandfather
amor [er-'mor] love
folha {'fo-l'yer] leaf

It has the sound of 'oo' in unstressed syllables and when it is on its own.
tomar [too-'mahr] to take
gato ['gah-too] cat

When it carries a tilde mark (õ) or precedes n, it has a nasal sound which we imitate in the same way as explained under ã. See also the paragraph dealing with nasal vowels and diphthongs.

u
This is always pronounced 'oo': **rua** [roo'er] street.

Oral diphthongs:

These are single vowel sounds resulting from the combination of two vowels (or two vowels pronounced as one syllable). An example of a diphthong in English is 'meat'. In Portuguese there are various combinations, notably:

ai = i as in 'my'	**vai** ['vah-ee] go, goes
au = ah'oo	**mau** ['mah'oo] bad
ao = ah'oh	**ao** ['ah'oh] at the, to the
ei = a as in 'tame'	**falei** [fer-'lay-ee] I spoke
eu = ay'oo *	**meu** [may'oo] my
oi = oy'e *	**foi** [foy'e] went
ou = o	**falou** [fer-'lo] he, you spoke
ui = oo'e	**fui** [foo'e] I went

* As with the nasal diphthongs that follow, it is difficult to reproduce these sounds on paper as they have no simple equivalents in English. Also note that the ai/ei sounds can be imitated by ah'ee and ay'ee sliding into the second vowel, with a little more emphasis on the first.

Note: when there is an accent over a diphthong you should treat the two vowels separately, *not* as a diphthong: **seu** is a diphthong but **céu** ['say-oo] is not.

Nasal vowels and diphthongs:

Whenever the vowels **a**, **e**, **i**, **o** and **u** precede **m** and **n**, they become nasal. If you have learned French, you should be familiar with the sound - for example, in *monter* or *environ*. It has already been pointed out that the italic n we use to imitate this should not be pronounced fully; if you make the sound properly through your nose, there ought not to be much likelihood of error.

The same applies to the nasal diphthongs **ão**, **ãe**, **ãi** and **õe**, which we imitate as ah'oo*n*, ah'e*n*, ah'e*n* and aw'i*n* respectively.

encanto [e*n*-'kahn-too] charm
jardim [zher-'dee*n*] garden
ontem ['o*n*-te*n*] yesterday
untar [oo*n*-'tahr] to grease
não [nah'oo*n*] no
limões [lee-'maw'i*n*sh] lemons

Consonants

These are pronounced as in English, with the following exceptions:

c
This sounds like s in 'silver` when it comes before **e** or **i**; it is hard ('k') as in 'cat' when coming before **a, o** and **u**, unless it bears a cedilla (ç) which changes the sound to ss. The combination **ch** must be pronounced as an English sh.
cinema [see-'nay-me*r*] cinema
comer [koo-'mayr] to eat
começar [koo-m*e*-'sahr] to begin
chave ['shah-v*e*] key

d
In Brazil, this is a harder sound almost as in English.

g
It sounds like the s in 'treasure', when coming before **e** or **i**. We imitate this by putting zh, but you must remember to pronounce it with your tongue further back from your teeth than in 'zoo'. Another similar sound is the French j, ge- or gi-.
geral [zhe*r*-'rahl] general
gigante [zhee-'ga*n*-t*e*] giant

It is hard, as in 'get', before **a, o, u** and preceding a consonant.
gordo ['gohr-doo] fat

When in the combination **gu**, before **e** or **i**, the **u** is not pronounced.
guerra ['gehr-re*r*] war
guitarra [gee-'tahr-re*r*] guitar

h
This is never sounded.

j

Like the s in 'treasure'; it precedes **a**, **o**, **u**, but hardly ever **e**.
jardim [zher-'dee*n*] garden
jóia ['zhoh-ye*r*] jewel

l

The final l is prolonged, but in Brazil it has a faint quality.
fácil ['fah-seel] easy ['fah-see'oo]

lh

Give this a liquid sound, like the lli in 'billiards'.
melhor [m*e*-'l'yohr] better
milho ['mee-l'yoo] maize

nh

Pronounced as the ni in 'onion': **minha** ['mee-n'ye*r*] mine.

qu

Has the sound of 'k', hard as in 'cat' – but the **u** is not pronounced before **e** or **i**.
qual [kwal] wish
quem [ke*n*] who

r

Has a soft sound, close to the Italian r in 'caro' or the second r in 'rare', when between vowels. It has a harder sound, like the well-rolled Scottish r or the first r in 'rare', when it is doubled or comes at the beginning of a word. At the end of a word or syllable it is prolonged still further. But in Brazil the final r is usually dropped.
barato [be*r*-'rah-too] cheap
carro ['kah-rroo] car
amor [e*r*-'mor] love

s

As in 'salt' when beginning a word, doubled or after a consonant. Between vowels it is less sibilant, like s in 'rose' or z in 'zebra'. The final s of a word or syllable sounds like sh in 'sheep'. Brazilians sound a final s more as we do in English.
sonho ['so-n'yoo] dream

rosa ['roh-ze*r*] rose
lápis ['lah-peesh] pencil
cesto ['say-shtoo] basket

t

Always as in 'tea'. In Brazil, like 'ch' - especially before **e** and **i**.

x

This has five sounds. It is like the English sh, when coming at the beginning of a word or between vowels. Also between vowels it can sound like s in 'some'. It has the sound of z when in the prefix **ex** plus a vowel, but is like ey'sh when **ex** is followed by a consonant. In words of foreign derivation it should be pronounced ks, as in English.
xadrez [she*r*-'draysh] chess
queixa ['kay-she*r*] complaint
trouxe [tros*e*] I brought
exército [ee-'zehr-see-too] army
explicar [ey'sh-plee-'kahr] to explain
taxi ['tah-ksee] taxi

z

Pronounce it as in 'zebra', except when it comes at the end of a word. A final **z** sounds like sh.
zanga ['za*n*-ge*r*] anger
fazer [fe*r*-'zayr] to do, to make
luz [loosh] light

Introduction

Bom dia. [bon'dee-er] Good morning.

Boa tarde. ['boh-er 'tahr-d] Good afternoon.

Boa noite. ['boh-er 'noyt] Good evening/good night.

Eu chamo-me Maria Fernanda Allen.
['ay'oo 'sher-moom]
    My name is . . . (I am called . . .).

Como se chama o senhor?
['kom-oo se 'sher-mer oo sen''yor]
    What is your name? (*addressing a man*).

Como se chama a senhora?
['kom-oo se 'sher-mer oo sen''yor-er]
    What is your name? (*addressing a woman*).

Como se chama você? ['kom-oo se 'sher-mer 'voh-seh]
    What is your name? (*casual 'you', either sex*).

Sou a sua professora. [so er 'soo-er proof''so-rer]
    I am your teacher.

Sou portuguesa. [so poor'too-'gay-zer]
    I am Portuguese.

O **senhor é inglês?** [oo sen''yor eh eeng-'laysh]
    Are you English? (*addressing a man*).

A **senhora é inglesa?** [er sen''yor-er eh eeng-lay-zer]
    Are you English? (*addressing a woman*).

Eu moro em Chelsea. ['ay'oo 'moh-roo e*n* . .]
I live in Chelsea.

Onde mora? [o*n*'d 'moh-re*r*]
Where do you live?

Fala Português? ['fah-le*r* poor-too-'gaysh]
Do you speak Portuguese?

Não? [nah'oo*n*] No?

Não faz mal. [nah-oo*n* fahsh mahl]
It does not matter.

Vamos agora aprender a falar português.
['ver-moosh e*r*-'goh-re*r* e*r*-pre*n*-'dair e*r* fe*r*-'lahr poor-too-
'gaysh]
We are now going to learn (to speak) Portuguese.

Bracketed translations should be taken merely as a literal
meaning of the idea expressed in the Portuguese idiom. Thus:

Idiomatic Portuguese	*Idiomatic English*
Precisa de ajuda?	Do you need any help?
	(Literally You need help?*)*
de dieta	on a diet
	(Literally of diet*)*

Chapter 1

In this first chapter you'll learn some very basic but extremely important elements of grammar, including:

- how to recognise whether a noun is masculine or feminine
- formation of the plural
- the articles - how to say 'the' and 'a'
- the present tense of '**ter**' ('to have'), together with personal pronouns ('I', 'you', 'he', 'she' etc)
- simple negative and interrogative forms

1 Nouns

All Portuguese nouns are either masculine or feminine; there is no neuter 'it'. Nouns and adjectives ending in **-o, -im, -om** and **-um** are generally masculine, while those ending in **-a, -ã, -gem, -dade, -ice, -ez, -ção, -são** and **-ude** are feminine. Nouns ending in **-r, -l** and **-e** are not necessarily masculine (as is often wrongly stated), for they have an equal chance of being feminine. For example:

a flor (f) the flower, but
o amor (m) love
a capital (f) the capital (city), but
o capital (m) the capital (money)
a noite (f) the evening/night, but
o perfume (m) the perfume

Learn more about the identification of gender in section 21.

The plural

The plural of nouns and adjectives is formed, in general, by adding **-s** to those ending in a vowel (a/e/i/o/u), and **-es** to those ending in a consonant. Those ending in **-m** change the **-m** to **-ns**. For other rules regarding the plural, see section 22.

2 The definite article

'The' agrees with the noun in gender and number, as seen in the examples given in section 1 above.

Masculine singular:	**o**	**o perfume**
Masculine plural:	**os**	**os perfumes**
Feminine singular:	**a**	**as noite**
Feminine plural:	**as**	**as noites**

Learn more about the definite article in section 50.

Exercise 1

This exercise doubles as a vocabulary list; learn what the words mean, then fill in the blanks with the appropriate definite article:

1	____ **rapariga**	the girl (in *Brazil:* **moça**)
2	____ **rapaz**	the boy
3	____ **escritório**	the office
4	____ **casa**	the house, home
5	____ **flores**	the flowers
6	____ **empregos**	the jobs, employment
7	____ **gatos**	the cats
8	____ **alunas**	the pupils
9	____ **mesa**	the table
10	____ **mesas**	the tables

IMITATED PRONUNCIATION (§2/Ex.1): oo; oo per-'foo-mer;
oosh; oosh per-'foo-mersh; er; er 'noy'e-ter; ersh; ersh 'noy'e-tersh.
rer-per-'ree-ger; 'moh-ser; rer-'pahsh; ish-kree-'toh-re'o; 'kah-zer;
flo'rsh; en-'pray-goosh; 'gah-toosh; er-'loo-nersh; 'may-ser;
'may-sersh.

3 The indefinite article

In Portuguese, 'a' and 'an' are translated as **um** before any
masculine singular noun, and **uma** before any feminine singular noun. Unlike English, these articles also have plural
forms: **uns** *(m pl)* and **umas** *(f pl)*, which are best translated
as 'some' or not translated at all. For example:

um homem (a man)   masculine singular (*m sing.*)
uma mulher (a woman)   feminine singular (*f sing.*)
uns homens (men, some men)
umas mulheres (women, some women)

Exercise 2

*Again, learn these new words and then fill in the blanks with the
appropriate indefinite article:*

1 ___	**viagem**	a trip
2 ___	**escritório**	an office
3 ___	**avião**	a plane
4 ___	**cidade**	a city, town
5 ___	**bilhete** *(m)*	a ticket
6 ___	**homens**	men
7 ___	**mulheres**	women
8 ___	**viagens**	trips, voyages, travels
9 ___	**escritórios**	offices
10 ___	**raparigas**	girls

IMITATED PRONUNCIATION (§3/Ex.2): oo*n;* 'oo-me*r,*
oon 'oh-me*n;* 'oo-me*r* mool-'yair; oo*n*sh; 'oo-me*r*sh;
oo*n*sh 'oh-me*n*sh; 'oo-me*r*sh mool-'yairsh vee-'ah-zhe*n;*
ish-kree-'toh-re'o; e*r*-vee-'ah-oo*n;* see-'dah-d*e;* beel-'yay-t*e;*
'oh-me*n*sh; mool-'yairsh; vee-'ah-zhe*n*sh; ish-kree-'toh-re'oosh;
re*r*-pe*r*-'ree-ge*r*sh.

PRACTISE!

*Study the following piece and its vocabulary list, then answer
the questions in the exercise. Answers will be found in the Key
at the end of the book.*

A senhora Smith é inglesa. Ela é de Londres, mas agora
mora em Lisboa. Ela tem um bom emprego como auditora
de uma grande companhia. Tem um escritório no Estoril.
O marido dela é um bom professor de inglês. Eu sou
portuguesa. Chamo-me Maria Helena. Sou do Algarve
mas agora moro em Lisboa porque sou médica em Lisboa.
Lisboa é a capital de Portugal e é uma linda cidade. Eu não
falo português mas não faz mal porque vou agora
aprender a falar português.

ela é de	she is from
em	in
como	as
grande	large (big, great)
no	in the
médica	doctor *(of medicine)*
não	no, don't, not
mas agora	but now (at present)
ela tem	she has
auditora	auditor
companhia	company
o marido dela	her husband
linda	beautiful
porque	because

Exercise P.1

Answer the following questions, basing your replies upon the piece you've just read.

1 A senhora Smith é portuguesa?
2 Onde mora agora?
3 Ela tem um bom emprego?
4 Como médica?
5 Onde tem ela o escritório?
6 Que faz o marido dela? (What does her husband do?)
7 A Maria Helena é de Lisboa'?
8 Que faz ela?
9 Lisboa é a capital de Espanha?
10 Londres é uma cidade linda?
11 Você fala português?
12 Você é (are you) professora (female teacher)?

Greetings, farewells and words of courtesy

Olá!	Hello!
Como está?	How are you?
Estou bem, obrigada *(Woman's reply)*	I'm well, thank you.
Estou bem, obrigado *(Man's reply)*	I'm well, thank you.
De nada	Not at all; It's OK.
Não tem de quê	Not at all; Don't mention it.
Adeus!	Goodbye! *(In Brazil:* **até logo!***)*
Até logo!	See you later!
Até amanhã!	See you tomorrow!
Faz favor	Please;
	(letting someone go in front of you) after you; please do;
	(shop assistant) Can I help you?
	(drawing someone's attention) Excuse me.
Por favor	Please.
Faça o favor de . . .	Please . . . *(more formal).*
Se faz favor . . .	If you please . . .
Desculpe!	Sorry!/Excuse me!
Com licença!	Excuse me! *(when reaching across someone, passing in front of people, entering or leaving a room . . . literally, 'With your permission')*

4 Present tense of verb 'ter' (to have)

First, a note in general about the Portuguese present tense: it translates the English present tense ('I do'), the present continuous ('I am doing') and the future ('I shall do') - though there is a future tense in Portuguese. The Portuguese present, with the help of **há** (see section 6), can even be used for the English perfect provided that the sentence refers to time: 'I have done (it) for two years'.

Here is the present tense of ter:

Singular

eu tenho	I have
tu tens	you have (*familiar*)
você tem	you have
o senhor tem	you have (*m formal*)
a senhora tem	you have (*f formal*)
ele tem	he has
ela tem	she has

Plural

nós temos	we have
vocês têm	you have (*familiar*)
os senhores têm	you have (*m formal*)
as senhoras têm	you have (*f formal*)
eles têm	they have (*m*)
elas têm	they have (*f*)

NOTE: 'you'
Portuguese has several forms of this personal (subject) pronoun with which you will need to become acquainted. Read the relevant notes in section 7; briefly, **tu** is the familiar form, **você** is neither familiar nor formal, **vocês** is the plural equivalent of both **tu** and **você**, while **o senhor** and **a senhora** are used when addressing men and women formally (plural forms **os senhores, as senhoras**).

IMITATED PRONUNCIATION (§4): 'ay'oo 'tern-yoo; too ten'sh; 'voh-seh ten; oo sen-'yor ten; er sen-'yor-er ten; ell ten; 'eh-ler ten; nosh 'tay-moosh; 'voh-sehs 'tay'ing; oosh sen''yorsh 'tay'ing; ersh sen''yor-ersh 'tay'ing; ellsh 'tay'ing; 'ehl-ersh 'tay'ing.

4a Expressions with the verb 'ter' which in English use the verb 'to be'

ter fome	to be hungry
ter sede	to be thirsty
ter frio	to be cold
ter calor	to be warm
ter sono	to be sleepy
ter razão	to be right
ter pressa	to be in a hurry
ter vinte anos	to be twenty years old

ter saudades to feel longing, nostalgia for, to miss - *e.g.*:
Tenho saudades de Portugal.
> I miss Portugal.

Another common expression is:
Que é que tem?
> What is the matter with you?

ter de or **ter que** expresses a strong necessity or obligation:

Tenho que terminar este trabalho.
> I have to finish this work.

Voce tem de partir imediatamente.
> You must leave immediately.

IMITATED PRONUNCIATION (§4a): tair fohm; said; 'free'oo; ker-'lohr; 'soh-noo; rer-'zah'oon; 'preh-ser, 'veen-t''eer-noosh; ser'oo-'dah-d'sh; poor-too-'gahl; kee''eh ke teng; 'tern-yoo ke terr-mee-'nahr esht trer-'bahl-yoo; 'voh-seh ten de per-'teer em-d''yah-ter-ment.

5 Affirmative, negative, interrogative forms

a) The affirmative 'yes' is **sim**:

Sim, tenho dinheiro.
　　Yes, I have (I do have) money.

b) **Não** means 'no', 'not', and 'to do' in the negative:

Não, não tenho dinheiro.
　　No, I have not (I don't have) any money.

c) To ask a question, you simply give an enquiring intonation to what would otherwise be a statement:

Fala inglês?
　　Do you speak English?
Tem troco?
　　Have you (any) change?
Que disse você?
　　What did you say?

NOTE: When the sentence begins with an interrogative pronoun or adverb, the subject pronoun usually comes after the verb, as in the example above. Otherwise it is constructed in the same way as the affirmative:

Você não quer mais vinho?
　　Don't you want any more wine?

NOTE: When 'to do' has a constructive meaning, it is translated by **fazer**, which also means 'to make':

Que faz?
　　What are you doing?
Ela não faz nada.
　　She doesn't do/isn't doing anything.

6 The verb 'haver'

This is a very important verb. **Haver** is used mainly in the third person singular, with the meaning of 'there is', 'there are', 'ago' and 'for' (relating to time). In this usage it corresponds to the French *il y a*, the Spanish *hay* and the Italian c'è. For example:

Há muita gente aqui.
There are a lot of people here.

Há quanto tempo está em Lisboa?
(For) how long have you been in Lisbon?

O avião partiu há cinco minutos.
The plane left five minutes ago.

Haver de fully conjugated in the present tense, plus the infinitive of another verb, expresses an action in the future. It implies a strong intention, equivalent to 'I will':

Hei-de ir áo Brasil.
I will go to Brazil.

Present tense

Singular

eu hei-de	I will . . .	
tu hás-de	you will . . .	*(familiar)*
você há-de	you will . . .	*(informal)*
ele há-de	he will . . .	
ela há-de	she will . . .	

Plural

nós havemos de	we will . . .	
vocês hão-de	you will . . .	*(familiar)*
eles hão-de	they will . . .	*(m)*
elas hão-de	they will . . .	*(f)*

IMITATED PRONUNCIATION (§6): ah 'm'ween-ter gent er-'kee; ah 'kwan-too 'ten-poo ish-'tah en leesh-'bo'er, oo er-ve-'ah'oon per-t''yoo ah 'seen-koo mee-'noo-toosh; er-'vair'd. 'ay'oo aide; too 'ahsh'de; 'voh-seh ah-de; el ah-de; 'eh-ler ah'de; nosh er-'vay-moosh'de; 'voh-sehs 'ah'oon -de; ellsh 'ah'oon-de; 'ehl-ersh 'ah'oon-de.

7 Subject pronouns

These you have already met in sections 4 and 6; they are the personal pronouns 'I', 'he', 'they', and so on. (Later, we come to another group of personal pronouns, the object pronouns 'me', 'him', 'them' etc.)

The Portuguese subject pronouns **eu** ('I'), **tu** ('you') and **nós** ('we') are frequently omitted except for the purpose of emphasis or because the verb ending indicates who is performing the action.

tu ('you', *familiar*) is used among friends, relatives, and in addressing children. It is seldom used in Brazil.

você ('you', *informal* not familiar) is used mainly between persons of the same age group or from employer to employee, teacher to student etc. It is widely used in Brazil.

vocês ('you', *plural*) *is* used both as the familiar and the informal form.

O senhor, a senhora, os senhores, as senhoras are the most polite forms of rendering 'you', when addressing a man, a woman, men, women. When talking to a mixed group of people, the masculine form is used.

Both **você** and **o senhor/a senhora** take the third person singular form of the verb, the same as **ele** ('he') and **ela** ('she'). **Vocês** and **os senhores/as senhoras** take the third person plural, the same as **eles/elas** ('they').

The word for 'you' may be omitted completely once the form of address has been established in a particular situation. For example:

Falas Português?
>   Do you *(familiar)* speak Portuguese?

Fala Português?
>   Do you *(informal* or *formal)* speak Portuguese?

There is another plural 'you' form, **vós**, but we shall ignore it in this course because it is no longer used except by older folk in northern Portugal, and is found only in classical texts, prayers etc. You will find it, with its verbal forms, in Hugo's *Portuguese Verbs Simplified*.

In referring to an individual who represents a group, a company, etc., use the plural 'you' pronoun, **vocês**, with the appropriate verbal form (sometimes the pronoun may be omitted):

Vocês têm os planos prontos?
>   Have you got the plans ready? (Are the plans ready'?)

A que horas abrem?
>   (At) What time do you open?

A group of men and women (or of male and female animate objects) will take the plural form in the masculine.

Ele ('he'), **ela** ('she'), **eles** ('they' *m*), **elas** ('they' *f*): 'it' is translated by **ele or ela** according to whether the noun referred to is masculine or feminine. Where there is some doubt, then use the masculine pronoun. In an impersonal context, such as 'It is important . . . ', there is no need to translate it at all.

Exercise 3

Translate the following (you should have learnt the vocabulary already – see Exercises 1 and 2, and Section 6):

1 Tenho.
2 Você tem?
3 Não temos.
4 Vocês têm.
5 Ela tem?
6 Os senhores não têm.
7 Eles não têm?
8 I have no money.
9 Have you (*f sing formal*) a ticket?
10 They (*m*) have good jobs.
11 Have you (*pl informal*) a house?
12 You (*sing familiar*) have an office.
13 We are hungry.
14 There is no table.
15 How long have you (*formal*) been speaking English?

CONVERSATION

Three short, simple dialogues

1

   A   Bom dia. O senhor tem cigarros ingleses com filtro?

   B   Agora não tenho, desculpe. Mas aquela loja à esquina tem cigarros ingleses, com certeza.

   A   Obrigado.

2

   A   Você tem tempo para um café?

   B   Sim, tenho, com muito prazer.

   A   Então vamos aqui ao lado. Têm um café muito bom e há pouca gente.

3

   A   Os seus amigos ainda têm o andar em Lisboa?

   B   Agora não, mas têm uma linda casa no Algarve, com um grande jardim e piscina.

   A   Que sorte! Quem me dera ter uma casa assim!

   B   Eu também.

Vocabulary

1

cigarros ingleses [see-'gah-rroosh een-'glay-shesh]	English cigarettes
com [ko*n*]	with
agora não [er-'goh-rer 'nah-oo*n*]	not at the moment
desculpe [d'sh-'kool- p*e*]	I'm sorry
mas [me*rsh*]	but
aquela [er-'kay-ler]	that (*f. sing*)
loja ['loh-zher]	shop
esquina [esh-'kee-ner]	corner
com certeza [ko*n* ser-'tay-zer]	definitely, certainly, for sure

2

tempo para ['te*n*-poo per'er]	time for
muito prazer [moo'i*n*-too prer-'zayr]	great pleasure
então [e*n*"tah'oon]	then, in that case
vamos aqui ao lado ['ver-moosh er-'kee ah'oo 'lah-doo]	let's go next door
pouca gente ['poh-ker 'zhe*n*-t*e*]	not many people, few people

3

Os seus amigos ainda têm o andar em Lisboa? [osh 'say'osh er-'mee-gosh er-'een-der 'tay'ing oo an-'dahr e*n* leesh-'boh-er]	Do your friends still have the flat in Lisbon?
linda ['lee*n*-der]	beautiful
grande ['grah*n*-de]	big, large
jardim [zher-'dee*n*]	garden
piscina [peesh-'see-ner]	swimming pool
que sorte! [k*e* 'sohr-t*e*]	what luck!, how fortunate!
quem me dera [ke*n* m' 'deh-rer]	how I wish . . .
assim [er-'ssi*n*]	like that
eu também ['ay'oo tah*n*-'ben]	me too, so would I

Chapter 2

Introducing two very important verbs, 'ser' and 'estar'
(both meaning 'to be'), with particular reference to their
present tenses. Other topics include:

* *adjectives, and how they must agree in number and gender*
  with the noun they belong to
* *important prepositions*
* *forms of address*

---

8 'Ser' and 'estar'

The irregular verbs **ser** [sair] and **estar** [ish-'tahr] both mean
'to be', but they have different rôles. In general, **ser** denotes
an inherent or permanent quality of 'being', and a profes-
sion or calling, even if *temporary*. It is wrong to say the verb
ser is permanent, and to leave the student to sort out the
confusion which will come later. There is nothing permanent about **sou um aluno** 'I am a student'; nor indeed about
sou um turista 'I am a tourist'. The same can be said for **sou
solteiro** 'I am single/a bachelor'. In short, **ser** is *what* you
are, or *who* you are. The following examples will clarify the
point:

Sou portuguesa. I (*f*) am Portuguese.
Lisboa é linda. Lisbon is beautiful.
Ele é casado. He is married.
Nós somos amigos. We are friends.

8a 'Ser' plus the preposition 'de'

Ser plus the preposition **de** denotes possession, origin. Where there is a possessive adjective or pronoun, **de** is omitted:

Eles são de Londres. They are from London.
Esta chave é do senhor Gomes. This key belongs to Mr Gomes.
Esta casa é minha. This house is mine.

Ser is also used for the passive voice, impersonal phrases, telling the time, and permanent location (a well-known place). For example:

Este trabalho é sempre feito por mim. This work is always done by me.
É importante. It is important.
É uma hora da tarde. It is 1.00pm.
Onde é o castelo de Windsor? Where is Windsor Castle?

8b 'Estar'

Estar is used when speaking of a temporary state or condition, action, and place.

Eles estão em Londres. They are in London. When comparing this example to the preceding, which uses **ser**, notice the prepositions are different: birthplace uses **de** and location uses **em**; this is another clue - if you see **em** you know that **estar** must be used.

Temporary state or condition
Ela está feia. She is looking ugly.
(But: **Ela é feia.** She is ugly.)
Nós estamos cansados. We are tired.

Estar plus the preposition **a** followed by the infinitive is used to express the present continuous tense. For example:

Eu estou a trabalhar. I am working.
(In Brazil, the present participle is used instead of the infinitive. Thus: **Eu estou trabalhando.**)

Estar com expresses the same meaning as **ter** in expressions such as:

Estou com fome (= Tenho fome) I am hungry.
Estou com sono (= Tenho sono) I am sleepy.
See also section 4a.

8c Present tenses

	ser	estar
eu (I)	sou	estou
tu (you *familiar*)	és	estás
você (you *informal*)	é	está
ele, ela (he, she)	é	está
nós (we)	somos	estamos
vocês (you *pl informal*)	são	estão
os senhores (you *formal m pl*)	são	estão
as senhoras (you *formal f pl*)	são	estão
eles, elas (they *m f*)	são	estão

Please refer to the subject pronouns given in section 7.

Sentences with the verbs **ser** and **estar**:

Ela é linda. She is beautiful.
Ela está linda. She is looking beautiful.
O homem é velho. The man is old.
O homem está velho. The man is getting old.
Elas são aborrecidas. They *(f pl)* are boring.
Elas estão aborrecidas. They *(f pl)* are bored.

Eu sou enganada por todos.
   I (*f sing*) am misled (cheated, taken for a ride) by every-
   one.
Eu estou enganada.
   I am mistaken.

IMITATED PRONUNCIATION (§8c): so; ehsh; eh; 'so-moosh;
'sah-oo*n* . . . ; ish-'to; ish-'tahsh; ish-'tah; ish-'te*r*-moosh;
ish-'tah-o*n* . . . ; 'lee*n*-de*r*; 'vehl-yoo; e*r*-boor-*r*e-'seed-e*r*sh;
e*n*-ge*r*-'nah-de*r*; poor 'to-doosh.

Exercise 4 (on **ser**)

*Study the list of words that follows an exercise before you
attempt translation.*

1 I (*f*) am English.
2 Are you the manager of this hotel?
3 He is boring.
4 She is a secretary.
5 This is very important.
6 We (*f*) are friends.
7 They (*m*) are old.
8 Are these the suitcases? (*meaning* your suitcases)
9 Estas malas não são minhas.
10 Isto é impossível.
11 Eu não sou secretária, sou professora.
12 Nós somos amigas.
13 Vocês são casados?

Vocabulary

inglesa [een-'glay-zer]	English (f)
gerente [je-'ren-te]	manager
deste ['daysh-te]	of this
hotel [o-'tel]	hotel
secretária [se-kre-'tah-ree-er]	secretary
isto ['eesh-too]	this
importante [een-poor''tan-te]	important
estas ['ehsh-tersh]	these
malas ['mah-lersh]	suitcases
minhas ['meen-yersh]	mine (f)
impossível [een-poss-'ee-vel]	impossible
casados [ker-'zah-doosh]	married

Exercise 5 (on estar)

1 I am in London.
2 Are you (f familiar) tired?
3 She is not at home.
4 We are working every day.
5 They (m) are mistaken.
6 The train is late.
7 Estou a comer.
8 Você está hoje em casa?
9 Nós não estamos enganados.
10 O senhor está com fome.
11 Elas estão lindas.
12 As raparigas estão prontas.

Vocabulary

Londres ['lon-dresh]	London
cansadas [kan-'sah-dersh]	tired (f pl)
em casa [en-'kah-ser]	at home
trabalhar [trer-berl-'yahr]	to work
todos os dias	every day
['to-doosh oosh 'dee-ersh]	
o comboio [oo kon-'boh'e-oo]	the train
	(In Brazil, 'train' is **trem**.)
atrasado [er-trer-'zah-doo]	late
comer [koo-'mayr]	to eat
hoje [o-zhe]	today
fome ['foh-me]	hunger
prontas ['pron-tersh]	ready (f pl)

PRACTISE!

Study the following piece and its vocabulary list, then answer the questions in the exercise.

NA ESPLANADA

It is 5 p.m. and people crowd the pavement cafés for tea or a cold drink. Complete strangers often share the same table. Paula makes her way to a table where just one man is sitting.

Paula	Está aqui alguém?
Homem	Não, não. Faz favor!
Paula	Obrigada. Está tanta gente!
Homem	É verdade! E está tanto calor!
Paula	*(calling the waiter)* Faz favor!
Criado	Um momento, se faz favor . . .
	Faz favor! Que deseja?
Paula	Um chá forte com leite, um pastel de nata e um copo de água.
Homem	Desculpe, você é inglesa?

Paula   Nâo, sou americana mas vivo há muito tempo na
Inglaterra.
(She reaches across for the sugar) Com licença! O
senhor é português?

Homem Não, sou brasiliero mas minha familia é portuguesa.
Estou aqui em negócios. E você?

Paula   Estou de férias e quero praticar o meu português.

Homem Fala muito bem.

Paula   Obrigada. Pode me dizer onde estão os lavabos?

Homem Sim, estão ali à sua direita.

Paula   Muito obrigada e adeus. Vou pagar a conta ao
balcão.

Homem Adeus e boas férias!

aqui	here
alguém	anybody, somebody
tanto/tanta	so much
gente *(f)*	people
verdade *(f)*	truth, true
calor *(m)*	heat, hot
que deseja	what would you like
chá *(m)*	tea
forte	strong
com	with
leite *(m)*	milk
pastel de nata	a kind of custard tart
copo de água *(m)*	a glass of water
mas vivo	but I live
vivo há muito tempo	I have lived for a long time
	(see section 6)
a minha familia	my family
em negócios	on business
de férias (em férias)	on holiday
e	and
quero	I want
praticar	to practise (to put into practice)
pode me dizer	can you tell me
lavabos	public lavatories
à sua direita	on your right
vou	I'm going
pagar ao balcão	to pay at the desk *(lit.* counter)
conta	bill

Exercise P. 2

Answer the questions, then have a go at re-enacting this scene with some friends or others in the class. Since your answers (which should of course be in Portuguese) are contained in the preceding text, we'll not include this exercise in the Key at the back of the book.

1 Que pergunta Paula ao homem? (What does Paula ask the man?)
2 Está pouca (=few) gente?
3 Está frio?
4 Que deseja a Paula?
5 Ela é portuguesa?
6 Ela vive há pouco tempo na Inglaterra?
7 O homem é americano?
8 O homem está de férias?
9 Porque (=why) está Paula em Portugal?
10 Onde estão os lavabos?
11 Onde vai ela pagar a conta?

9 Adjectives

Adjectives agree in gender and number with the noun they qualify and they usually follow it. For example: **a língua portuguesa** the Portuguese language. As with nouns, the masculine ending of an adjective (**o**) changes to **a**, if the noun is feminine. If it ends in **s**, **z**, **r**, you add **a**. Adjectives ending in other consonants or **e** do not change in the feminine. In the plural adjectives behave like nouns. For additional rules see sections 21 and 22.

When the adjective precedes the noun, its meaning may be modified. For example:

um homem pobre a poor man (meaning he has no money)
um pobre homem a poor man (a man to be pitied on account of some misfortune)

Grande before a noun usually means 'great'. When it follows a noun, it means 'big' or 'large'. For example:

um grande homem a great man (meaning distinguished)
um homem grande a big man (referring to his physique)

But there are a number of other adjectives which preferably are placed before the noun:

bom/boa good
belo/bela beautiful
mau/má bad
longo/longa long
breve soon, short
muito/muita* much
muitos/muitas many

Note also that the ordinal numbers usually precede the noun, as in English: **no terceiro dia** on the third day.

The adjectives in Portuguese often serve as past participles which also agree in number and gender with the subject: **elas estão cansadas** they are tired.

* **Muito** as an adverb, meaning 'very much' or 'very', is invariable.

10 Main prepositions

de	of, from
em	in, on, at
a	at, to
por	for, by, through
para	for, to, in order to *(See section 48)*

Some of these prepositions combine with the articles as follows:
de plus **o, a, os, as** becomes **do, da, dos, das** 'of the', 'from the'.

de plus the indefinite article becomes **dum, duma, duns, dumas** 'of a', 'of some' (although in this case they could also be separated).

em plus the above becomes: **no, na, nos, nas** 'in the', 'on the', 'at the'.

num, numa, nuns, numas 'in a', 'in some', etc (sometimes separated).

a plus the definite article becomes: **ao, à, aos, às** 'to the', 'at the'. (It does not combine with the indefinite article.)

Por plus the definite article becomes: **pelo, pela, pelos, pelas** 'by the', etc. It does not combine with any other part of speech.

Para does not combine with any part of speech.

The first three prepositions **(de, em, a)** also join demonstrative adjectives; for example, **nesta** 'in this' (*f*), **disto** 'of/from this' (neuter). They also join 3rd persons of object pronouns, e.g. **dele** 'of/from him', **nelas** 'in them' - **delas** (*f pl*), and they combine with **aqui, ali** to give **daqui** 'from here', **dali** 'from there', etc.

IMITATED PRONUNCIATION (§10): d*e*; e*n*; e*r*, poohr; 'pe*r*-re*r*, doo, de*r*, doosh, de*r*sh; doo*n*, 'doo-me*r*, doo*n*sh; 'doo-me*r*sh; noo, ne*r*, noosh, ne*r*sh; noo*n*, 'noo-me*r*, noo*n*sh; 'noo-me*r*sh; 'ah'oo*n*, ah, 'ah'oo*n*sh, ahsh; 'pehl-oo, 'pehl-e*r*, 'pehl-oosh, 'pehl-e*r*sh.

Possessive case

The preposition **de** and its combined forms indicate the possessive case in Portuguese. For example:

Mary's house **A casa da Maria.**

Please refer to section 46.

Exercise 6

Translate the following:

1 The book is on the table.
2 The woman is at the door.
3 She is going through the park.
4 Uncle Tom's office.
5 I am on the (at the) telephone.
6 The water is in the glass.
7 I am here on holiday.
8 Vamos ao mercado.
9 Vou para casa.
10 Ela está na casa de banho.
11 Numa situação como esta.
12 Ele entrou pela janela.
13 Falo do acidente.
14 Ele deu o dinheiro ao rapaz.

Vocabulary

livro ['lee-vroo]	book
mesa ['may- se*r*]	table
porta ['pohr-te*r*]	door
ela vai ['eh-le*r* 'vah-ee]	she is going
parque *(m)* [park]	park
tio Tomás ['tee-oo too-'mahsh]	uncle Tom
telefone *(m)* [oo te-'le-foh-n*e*]	telephone
mercado [m*e*r-'kah-doo]	market
água ['ah-goo'e*r*]	water
copo['koh-poo]	cup
vou [voh]	I am going
casa ['kah-ze*r*]	home, house
casa de banho [be*r*n'yoo]	bathroom *(Br:banheiro)*
como esta ['koh-moo 'ehsh-te*r*]	like this (one)
situação [see-too-e*r*-'sa''oo*n*]	situation
ele entrou [el e*n*-'troh]	he came in
janela [zhe*r*-'neh-le*r*]	window
falo do . . . ['fah-loo doo]	I speak about the . . .
acidente [e*r*-see-'de*n*-te]	accident
ele deu [el day'oo]	he gave

Directions

Here are some basic responses to your question:
Pode me dizer, por favor, qual é o melhor caminho para . . . ?
Can you tell me, please, which is the best way to . . . ?

vá . . .	continue . . .
sempre a direito	straight on
sempre em frente	straight on
vire/volta à direita	turn to your right
vire/volta à esquerda	turn to your left
atravesse . . .	cross . . .
a rua	the street
os semáforos	the traffic lights
a rotunda	the roundabout
a passadeira de peões	zebra crossing
a passagem de peões	pedestrian crossing

Note that **a direito** (no accent on **a**, and **direito**) is used for 'straight on', while 'to your right'/'on the right' is **à direita**. Getting this wrong could make a big difference to your journey!

11 Forms of address

Sr stands for **Senhor** 'Mr'. **Sra** is the written abbreviation for **Senhora** 'Mrs'. When addressing a married woman, you use her Christian name preceded by Senhora Dona (Sra D.). In Brazil, just 'Dona' is sufficient. If you do not know her Christian name, then Senhora (Sra) plus her surname is the usual form of address. Use the abbreviated form when writing. Domestic helpers and tradespeople are normally addressed as Senhor/Senhora plus their Christian name. In Brazil, **Seu** is a common way of addressing male tradespeople (for example: 'Seu José'). Unmarried women (up to a certain age) may be addressed as **Menina** or just by their first name. In some cases Menina is used when addressing shopkeepers, switchboard girls, and so on. In Brazil, **Senhorita** would be used instead.

The student is advised to listen well to Portuguese people addressing each other in private and public places, before attempting to venture through the maze of Portuguese forms of address, with their various degrees of formality. (See Sections 4 & 7 for notes on 'you'.)

When addressing a doctor (medicine, law, PhD), **Senhor doutor** (Sr Dr) is used. For example: **Como está o Senhor doutor?** How are you, doctor? (**Senhora doutora** for a woman doctor). When addressing an engineer (university level) use **Senhor engenheiro** (Sr Eng). An architect (university level) is **Senhor arquitecto** (Sr Arq).

CONVERSATION

Um encontro/A meeting

Sr Smith	Olá Dona Linda. Como está?
Sra Pereira	Estou bem, obrigada. E você?
Sr Smith	Bem, obrigado.
Sra Pereira	Então por aqui?
Sr Smith	Sim, estou aqui há dois dias, em negócios.
Sra Pereira	E quanto tempo vai ficar em Lisboa?
Sr Smith	Vou ficar uma semana, pelo menos. Estou na casa dos meus amigos Bosomworth. Você lembra-se deles?
Sra Pereira	Sim, muito bem, por causa do nome. Creio que o nome deles quer dizer em Português, 'peito de valor'. Que cómico!
Sr Smith	Não é mais cómico que o seu, que quer dizer em Inglês 'beautiful peartree'.
Sra Pereira	Bem, é uma questão de opinião. Ah, aqui vem a minha amiga Angélica! Angélica, apresento-lhe o Sr. Tomás Smith . . . Doutora Angélica dos Santos da Purificação.
Sr Smith	Muito prazer, minha senhora.
Dra Santos da P.	Igualmente.
Sr Smith	Desculpe, por favor repita o seu nome e devagar. Não compreendi bem.
Dra Santos da P.	Angélica dos Santos da Purificação.
Sr Smith	Que pureza, senhora doutora!
Sra Pereira	Bem, desculpe Tomás, mas temos que nos ir embora. Estamos com muita pressa. Telefone-me. Adeus.
Sr Smith	Adeus Dona Linda e Doutora Angélica. Até breve.

TRANSLATION

Mr Smith Hello (Mrs) Linda. How are you?

Mrs Pereira I am very well, thank you. And you?

Mr Smith Well, thank you. (*Notice a man says* obrigado *and a woman says* obrigada)

Mrs Pereira Fancy meeting you here. (*literally* Are you here then?)

Mr Smith Yes, I have been here two days, **on business.**

Mrs Pereira And how long are you going to stay **(are you staying)** in Lisbon?

Mr Smith I am going to stay **(am staying)** for one week, **at least.** I am at my friends the Bosomworths' house. Do you remember them?

Mrs Pereira Yes, very well, because of their name. I believe their name (*literally* the name of them) means in Portuguese, 'peito de valor'. How funny!

Mr Smith No more than yours which means in English, 'beautiful peartree'.

Mrs Pereira Well, it is a matter of opinion. Ah, here comes my friend Angela. Angela. Let me introduce (to you) Mr Thomas Smith ... Dr Angela dos Santos da Purificação.

Mr Smith Pleased to meet you.

Santos da P. Likewise. (*literally* Equally.)

Mr Smith I am sorry, please repeat your name, and slowly. I didn't understand (it) well.

Santos da P. Angela of the Saints of the Purification.

Mr Smith What purity, dear doctor!

Mrs Pereira Well, I am sorry but we (shall have to) have to go. **We are in a hurry. Ring me up.** Good-bye.

Mr Smith Good-bye Linda and Dr Angela. See you soon.

The Portuguese present tense translates the:

English present simple tense (e.g. I stay); English present continuous tense (e.g. I am staying); English future with intention tense (e. g. I am *going to* stay); English future tense (e.g. we shall have to go).

See also section 32 *Other ways of expressing the future.*

The Portuguese present tense also translates the English perfect tense in sentences using **há** (see explanation on the uses of **há** in section 6):

Estou aqui há dois dias.
> I have been here for two days (lit. 'I am here there are two days').

Please repeat the following words and expressions from this conversation:

em negócios [en ne-'goh-see-oosh]	on business
pelo menos ['pay-loo 'may-noosh]	at least
lembra-se de . . . ? ['lenbrerse de]	do you remember . . . ?
creio que ['kray-o ke]	I believe
quer dizer [kehr dee-'zayr]	it means
apresento-lhe [er-prezen-too-l'ye]	I introduce to you
muito prazer ['moo'in-too prer-'zayr]	(It's a) great pleasure, how do you do?
igualmente* (ee-'gwahl-men-te)	likewise

* This is a useful little word that is used when reciprocating a wish or returning a compliment, and avoids repeating 'Muito prazer', 'Boa sorte' (Good luck), Feliz Natal' (Happy Christmas) etc.

Chapter 3

In this unit you are introduced to the present tenses of three regular verbs, one from each conjugation: **'falar', 'comer', 'abrir'.** *You'll also learn about:*

- *interrogatives ('who?', 'when?', 'why?' etc)*
- *relative pronouns ('who', 'which', 'whose' etc)*
- *demonstrative adjectives and pronouns ('this', 'that', 'these', 'those')*

12 Regular verbs

There are three conjugations which end respectively in **-ar, -er, -ir.** The part of the verb which precedes these terminations is called the *stem.* To conjugate any verb belonging to its respective conjugation all you have to do is to preserve the stem and add the appropriate endings as shown below. The endings are given in bold type. These must be learned because they indicate who is performing the action, since the personal pronoun is often omitted.

Present tense

	falar	**comer**	**abrir**
	(to speak)	(to eat)	(to open)
eu (I)	fal**o**	com**o**	abr**o**
tu (you *familiar*)	fal**as**	com**es**	abr**es**
você (you *informal*)	fal**a**	**come**	abr**e**
ele, ela (he, she)	fal**a**	com**e**	abr**e**

nós (we)	fal**amos**	com**emos**	abr**imos**
vocês (you *pl informal*)	fal**am**	com**em**	abr**em**
eles, elas (they *m, f*)	fal**am**	com**em**	abr**em**

IMITATED PRONUNCIATION: 'fah-loo, 'fah-lersh, 'fah-le*r*, fe*r*-le*r*-moosh, 'fah-law*n*; 'ko-moo, 'koh-m*e*sh, 'koh-m*e*, koo-'meh-moosh, 'koh-me*n*; 'ah-broo, 'ah-br*e*sh, 'ah-br*e*, e*r*-'bree-moosh, 'ah-br*e*n.

Exercise 7

(see vocabulary below)

1 Procuramos uma casa.
2 Eles não falam Português muito bem, mas compreendem   tudo.
3 Ela nunca aceita o meu convite.
4 Que toma o senhor?
5 Ele abre a janela.
6 Estudo todos os dias.
7 Vocês não comem muito.
8 Parto às nove horas.
9 Os senhores trabalham muito.
10 As senhoras compram os bilhetes.

Vocabulary

procurar [proo-koo-'rahr]	to look for
muito bem [moo'i*n*-too be*n*]	very well
compreender [ko*n*-pre-e*n*-'dayr]	to understand
perceber [pe*r*-se*r*-'bayr]	to understand
tudo ['too-doo]	everything
nunca ['noo*n*-ke*r*]	never
aceitar [e*r*-sa-'tahr]	to accept
meu ['may-oo]	my (*also* mine)
convite [ko*n*-'vee-t*e*]	invitation
que [k*e*]	what

tomar [too-'mahr]	to take, to have food or drink
estudar [ish-too-'dahr]	to study
todos os dias ['to-doosh oosh 'dee-ersh]	every day
partir [per-'teer]	to leave, to depart
às nove horas [ahsh 'noh-ve 'oh-rersh]	at nine o clock
muito ['mween-too]	very much, a lot
comprar [kon-'prahr]	to buy

Exercise 8

Translate into Portuguese:

1 My brother is looking for a job in Mozambique.
2 He is learning Portuguese.
3 Do you need help?
4 I accept your invitation with pleasure.
5 They drink and smoke too much.
6 The train leaves on schedule.
7 He is selling his car.
8 Today I am not buying anything.
9 My sister does not eat at one o'clock.
10 She is on a diet.

Vocabulary

meu irmão ['may-oo eer-'mah'oon]	my brother
Moçambique [moo-san-'bee-ke]	Mozambique
aprender [er-pren-'dayr]	to learn
precisar de [pre-see-'zahr de]	to need
ajuda [er-'joo-der]	help
seu ['say-oo]	your (formal)
beber [be-'bayr]	to drink
fumar [foo-'mahr]	to smoke
demasiado [de-mer-zee-'ah-doo]	too much
partir [per-'teer]	to leave

à tabela [ah te*r*-'bay-le*r*]	on time, on
(*In Brazil:* **no horário certo**)	schedule
vender [ve*n*-'day*r*]	to sell
carro ['kahr-roo]	car
nada ['nah-de*r*]	nothing
minha irmã ['mee-n'ye*r* eer-ma*n*]	my sister
à uma hora [ah 'oo-me*r* 'oh-re*r*]	at one o'clock
de dieta [d*e* dee-'ay-te*r*]	on a diet

PRACTISE!

Study the following piece and its vocabulary list (also check back to the section 'Directions'), then answer the questions in the exercise.

A senhora Smith procura um banco e Centro de Turismo. . .

Sra. Smith O senhor desculpe, dizia-me por favor se há um banco aqui perto?

Transeunte Sim, há. Fica a dois minutos daqui. A senhora vai por aqui, sempre a direito e depois de passar uma garagem vê logo o banco.

Sra. Smith Obrigada. Quero também ir ao Centro de Turismo. Onde fica?

Transeunte Fica um pouco longe daqui. É melhor a senhora apanhar um táxi. A praça de táxis está ali à sua esquerda depois de virar aquela esquina.

Sra. Smith E eles sabem onde está o Centro de Turismo?

Transeunte Claro, minha senhora, eles conhecem Lisboa como a palma da mão.

Sra. Smith Muito obrigada.

Transeunte De nada!

dizia-me	would you tell me
se há	if there is
um banco	a bank
perto	near
aqui perto	nearby
fica	it is (situated) (see **ficar,** to stay/remain/be/be situated, p. 94)
sim, há	yes, there is (one)
vai por aqui	(you) go this way
e depois de passar	and after you pass
uma garagem	a garage
vê logo	you see straight away
quero	I want (I would like)
também	also, too
ir ao . . .	to go to the . . .
Centro de Turismo	Tourist Office
onde fica	where is it
um pouco longe daqui	not far from here (lit 'a little far . . . ')
melhor	better
apanhar	to catch (in this case, to take)
praça de táxis (f)	taxi rank
ali	there
aquela esquina	that corner
e eles sabem . . . ?	do they know . . . ? (verb **saber**)
claro	naturally (= but of course)
conhecem	they know (see **saber, conhecer** p. 101)
como a palma da mão	like the palm of (their) hand (cf. 'back' in English idiom)

Exercise P. 3

Complete the following sentences (for answers, see Key):
Desculpe, ___ se ___ um banco aqui ___? Fica a ___ ___
___. A senhora vai ___ ___, sempre ___ ___ e depois de ___
uma garagem ___ ___ o banco. Quero também ___ ___
Centro de Turismo. Onde ___? Fica ___ ___ longe daqui. É
___ a senhora ___ um táxi. A praça de táxis ___ ___ à sua
___ depois de ___ aquela ___. E eles ___ onde ___ o Centro
de Turismo? ___, minha senhora, eles ___ Lisboa como ___
___ ___ ___.

13 Interrogatives and relative pronouns

como . . . ? adverb 'how . . . ?':

Como está?
How are you? *(sing.)*
Como se chama?
What is your name? *(lit.* How are you called?*)*
Como se diz 'table' em português?
How do you say 'table' in Portuguese?
A como estão as peras?
How much are the pears?

como conjunction 'as', 'like':

Ela é como a mãe.
She is like her mother.
. . . como eu não queria dizer . . .
. . . as I did not want to say . . .

quando . . . ? adverb 'when . . . ?':

Quando vai ao Brasil?
When are you going to Brazil?

quando conjunction 'when':

Quando ele falou comigo . . .
When he spoke with me . . .

onde . . . ? adverb 'where . . . ?':

Onde moram os senhores?
Where do you *(pl. formal)* live?
De onde vem?
Where are you coming from?
Por onde é a saida?
Where is the way out?

Note also **aonde?** and **para onde?**, 'where to?'.

quem . . . ? interrogative and relative pronoun 'who . . . ?',
'whom . . . '/'whose . . . ':

Quem foi que faz isto?
> Who (was it that) did/made this?

De quem é esta caneta?
> Whose pen is this?

Não foi ele quem me disse . . .
> It was not he who told me . . .

porque . . . ?, por que adverb and conjunction 'why . . . ?',
'for what (reason)?':

Porque é que ele comprou esta casa?
> Why did he buy this house? (*lit* Why is it that he
> bought)

Por que motivo . . . ?
> For what reason . . . ?

Note also **porque não?** 'why not?'; **porquê** adverb 'why';
porque conjunction 'because'.

que . . . ?, o que . . . ? interrogative pronouns 'what . . . ?',
'which . . . ?':

Que diz você? O que foi que ele faz?
> What are you saying? What was it that he did?

Que rua?
> Which street?

que relative pronoun 'that', 'which', 'whom':

O jantar que tive . . .
> The dinner (which) I had . . .

A mulher que você viu falar comigo . . .
> The woman whom you saw speaking to me . . .

Note also **que** in exclamations such as **Que chatice!** 'What a
nuisance!' (slang), and also the interrogative pronoun (used
on its own) **Quê?** 'What?'.

quanto . . . ? adverb, pronoun, adjective 'how much . . . ?':

Quanto custa?
How much does it cost?
Só Deus sabe quanto ela sofreu.
God alone knows how much she has suffered.

Note also: **quanto mais que** . . . 'particularly/specially as . . .', 'because . . .' and **quanto a** . . . 'as to/for . . .' (= in respect of).

quantos/quantas . . . ? (*m/f*) 'how many . . . ?':

Quantos quartos?
How many bedrooms?
Quantas libras deseja trocar?
How many pounds do you want to change?

qual, quais interrogative and relative pronoun, adjective, conjunction 'which', 'which one', 'who', 'whom', 'what', 'that' (denotes a preference, a limited number or emphasizes the subject):

Qual é o melhor hotel em Londres?
Which is the best hotel in London?
Quais são as calças que prefere?
Which are the trousers (that) you prefer?
A irmã do meu amigo, a qual escreveu um livro muito controverso.
My friend's sister, (the one) who wrote a very controversial book.

Note also: **cada qual** 'each one', 'each person', and **tal qual** . . . 'just like . . .'

Other relative pronouns are **cujo** (*m*), **cuja** (*f*), and their respective plural forms **cujos** and **cujas** 'whose', 'of which', 'of whom':

A minha secretária, cuja mãe vive América do Norte, vai-se embora.
My secretary, whose mother lives in North America, is going away.
A sua carta, cujo conteúdo me surpreendeu . . .
Your letter, the contents of which surprised me . . .

IMITATED PRONUNCIATION (§13): 'ko-moo; 'kwan-doo; 'on-de; ken; poor'-'ke; ke, oo ke 'kwan-too; 'kwan-toosh, 'kwan-tersh; kwal, 'kwa'eesh; 'koo-zhoo, 'koo- zher, 'koo-zhoosh, 'koo-zhersh.

Exercise 9

Translate the following:

1 Qual é a estação mais próxima daqui?
2 Qual é a sua morada? (Also: 'endereço', 'direção')
3 Ela nunca faz o que eu quero.
4 Porque não vai de automóvel?
5 Creio que é muito longe.
6 Como vão os seus negócios?
7 Não sei a quem devo pagar.
8 Where are you going?
9 How much do I owe?
10 You haven't told me (what is) your name.
11 What did you say?
12 Who is that handsome man?
13 When are you going to France?
14 The keys (that) she gave me are not mine.

Vocabulary

estação [ish-ter-'sah-oon]	station
a mais próxima ['mah-ish 'proh-see-mer]	nearest *(f sing)*
daqui [der-'kee]	to here (from here)
morada [moo-'rah-der]	address
nunca ['noon-ker]	never
faz [fahsh]	makes, does
quero ['keh-roo]	I want
vai ['vah-ee]	go, goes
automóvel [ah'oo-too-'moh-vel]	car
creio ['kray-oo]	I believe

longe ['lon-zhe]	far
vão ['vah-oon]	go *(pl)* are going
seus ['say-oosh]	your *(formal pl)*
negócios [ne-'goh-see-oosh]	business *(pl)*
devo ['deh-voo]	I should / must; do I owe
(from **dever,** ought to, should, must; *also:* to owe)	
pagar [per-'gahr]	to pay
não me disse	you haven't told me
[nah'oon me 'dee-ser]	
disse? ['dee-ser]	did you say?
aquele [er-'kay-le]	that (over there)
lindo ['leen-doo]	handsome *(m)*
simpático ['seen-'pah-te-koo]	handsome *(m)*
a França ['fran-sser]	to France
as chaves ['shah-vesh]	the keys
ela deu-me ['eh-ler day'oom]	she gave me

14 Demonstrative adjectives and pronouns

this   these

este *m sing*   **estes** *m pl*
esta *f sing*   **estas** *f pl*
isto *indeterminate*

that *(near to person addressed)*   those

esse *m sing*   **esses** *m*
essa *f sing*   **essas** *f pl*
isso *indeterminate*

that *(over there)*   those

aquele *m sing*   **aqueles** *m pl*
aquela *f sing*   **aquelas** *f pl*
aquilo *indeterminate*

The demonstrative adjectives and pronouns combine with the prepositions **de** and **em**, and the demonstrative adjective **aquele/aquela** also combines with the preposition **a**. For example:

nesta = **em** + **esta** in this, on this, at this (*f sing*)
daquele = **de** + **aquele** of that (*m sing*)
àquela = **a** + **aquela** to that, at that (*f sing*)
isto, isso, aquilo are used in place of nouns, when the gender of the noun is not known or indeterminate.

IMITATED PRONUNCIATION (§14) 'aysh-te; 'aysh-tesh; 'esh-ter; 'esh-tersh; 'ish-too; 'ay-se; 'ay-sesh; 'es-ser; 'es-sersh; 'e-soo; er-'kay-le; er-'kay-lesh; er-'keh-ler; er-'keh-lersh; er-'kee-loo;

Exercise 10

Translate the following:

1 Aquela loja à esquina.
2 Vamos àquela praia.
3 O que é isto?
4 Isto é um computador.
5 Por favor feche essa porta.
6 Este é o meu marido e aquele é o meu filho.
7 Estas chaves não são minhas.
8 This house is large.
9 What is that? *(closer to the person addressed)*
10 I do not want those *(over there)* books.
11 This is impossible.
12 He is in that hotel.
13 This suitcase is that man's (belongs to that man).
14 The tickets are in this handbag.

Vocabulary

praia ['prah-yer]	beach
computador [kon-poo-ter-'dor]	computer
feche [fay-she]	shut *(imperative form)*
meu marido ['may-oo mer-'ree-doo]	my husband
filho ['fee-l'yoo]	son
mala ['mah-ler]	suitcase *(also handbag)*
mala de senhora ['de sen-'yor-er]	lady's handbag
carteira [ker-'tay-rer]	handbag, wallet
grande ['gran-de]	large *(also big, great, grand)*

CONVERSATION

Um telefonema/A telephone call

Brrr ... Brrr ... Brrr ... Brrr...

Maria Estou.

António Está lá? É a Maria?

Maria Sou sim. Quem fala?

António Daqui fala o António. Bom dia, como está?

Maria Bem, obrigada. E você e sua familia?

António Menos mal, obrigado. Estou muito cansado. Ontem à noite voltei de Londres.

Maria E então teve férias boas?

António Sim, mas o tempo estava péssimo.

Maria Você fez muitas compras?

António Não muitas. Está tudo tão caro! Mas comprei uma lembrança para você que, infelizmente, se quebrou na viagem.

Maria	Não faz mal. Você é muito amável. Agradeço--lhe da mesma maneira.
António	Aonde vai passar as férias este ano?
Maria	Estou a pensar em ir a Londres também.
António	Fala inglês?
Maria	Não muito bem, mas faço-me compreender.
António	Londres é uma grande cidade, e linda, mas está sempre a chover. Você terá de levar um guarda-chuva.
Maria	Claro.
António	Então, Maria, que há de novo? E sua irmã Emilia? Que é feito dela?
Maria	Mas eu não tenho nenhuma irmã.
António	Você não se chama Maria dos Anjos da Silva?
Maria	Não, chamo-me Maria da Conceição Lopes.
António	Desculpe, enganei-me no número.

TRANSLATION

Maria	Hello? (*literally* 'I am').
António	Hello? (*literally* 'Are you there?') Is that you, Maria?
Maria	Yes, it's me. Who is that speaking?
António	António speaking (*literally* 'from here speaks António'). Good morning, how are you?
Maria	Well, thank you. And you and your family?
António	Not too badly, thank you. I am very tired. Last night (*literally* 'yesterday night') I returned from London.
Maria	And did you have good holidays?
António	Yes, but the weather was awful.

Maria	Did you do much shopping? (*literally* 'purchases')
António	Not much. (*literally* 'not many'). Everything is so expensive! But I bought a gift for you which, unfortunately, has got broken during the trip.
Maria	It doesn't matter. You are very kind. Thank you all the same.
António	Where are you going to spend your holidays this year?
Maria	I am thinking of going to London too.
António	Do you speak English?
Maria	Not very well, but I make myself understood.
António	London is a great city, and beautiful, but it is always raining. You will have to take an umbrella.
Maria	Naturally.
António	Well, Maria - what news? (*literally* 'What is there which is new?') And what about your sister Emilia? What has happened to her?
Maria	But I don't have a sister.
António	Are you not (*literally* 'don't you call yourself') Maria dos Anjos da Silva?
Maria	No. My name is (*literally* 'I call myself/I am called') Maria da Conceicao Lopes.
António	Oh I am sorry. I have the wrong number. (*literally* 'I made a mistake in the number').

Please repeat the following words and expressions from this conversation:

menos mal ['may-noosh mahl] not too bad (badly)

ontem à noite [on-ten ah 'noy-te] last night (*literally* 'yesterday at night')

então [en-'tah-oon] well, well then, so (*frequently used*)

férias boas ['feh-ree-ersh 'boh-ersh] good holidays (*or* **boas férias**)

infelizmente [een-feh-leesh-'men-te] unfortunately

Não faz mal. ['nah-oon fahsh mahl] It doesn't matter.

É muito amável. [eh 'mween-too er-'mah-vel] You are (*or* he/she is) very kind.

Agradeço-lhe. [er-grer-'dav-soo-l'ye] (I) thank you.

da mesma maneira [der 'maysh-mer mer-'nay-rer] all the same, in the same way

este ano [aysh-t'er-noo] * this year

claro ['klah-roo] of course, certainly, obviously, it goes without saying, etc (*very much in use*)

Que há de novo? [kee ah de 'no-voo] What is new? What (is the) news?

Que é feito dela? [kee'eh f'ay-too 'deh-ler] What has happened to her? What has she been doing?

Enganei-me. [en-ger-'nay-me] I made a mistake.

*Note that when a word ends in the vowel **e** and the following word begins with a vowel, the **e** stops being mute and takes on the sound of **ee** adjoining the following vowel. This is something in Portuguese pronunciation which the student must be aware of. The words are run together in what sounds like a very long word. When the word ends in a consonant and the next starts with a vowel, those two words are also joined in pronunciation, the final **s** (which normally has the sound of **sh**) taking on the sound of **z**.

Chapter 4

Now you will find out about the possessive adjectives and pronouns ('my', 'mine', 'your', 'yours' and so on), as well as:

• cardinal and ordinal numbers
• time expressions
• days, months, seasons and greetings

15 Possessive adjectives and pronouns

| | Thing(s) possessed | | | |
	m sing	f sing	m pl	f pl
my, mine	o meu	a minha	os meus	as minhas
your, yours (famil)	o teu	a tua	os teus	as tuas
your, yours (form)	o seu	a sua	os seus	as suas
his/her(s)/its	o seu	a sua	os seus	as suas
our, ours	o nosso	a nossa	os nossos	as nossas
your, yours	o vosso	a vossa	os vossos	as vossas
their, theirs	o seu	a sua	os seus	as suas

Since the forms **seu, sua, seus, suas** mean 'his, her/hers, their, theirs' as well as 'your, yours' (*formal*), to avoid ambiguity the forms **dele, dela, deles, delas** (*literally* 'of him', 'of her', 'of them') are often used instead. For example:

o seu lápis his/her/your pencil. But:
o lápis dele his pencil, **o lapis dela** her pencil

In the plural:
as suas casas his/her/your/ their houses. But:
as casas deles their houses, **as casas dela** her houses

You will have noticed that the **dele, dela, deles, delas** forms agree in number and gender with the subject noun ('he', 'she' etc.), also that they come *after* the object ('houses').

The definite article precedes a possessive adjective but it can be left out when speaking of close relatives. It is often omitted in Brazil. The possessive pronouns (mine, etc) do not require an article except when emphasizing ownership. Unlike English usage, the possessive adjective can be omitted in Portuguese when there is no doubt about the ownership. A common instance is in referring to parts of the body or personal clothing. For example:

Vou lavar as mãos. [voh ler-'vahr ersh 'mah-oonsh]
    I am going to wash my hands.
Vista o casaco. ['vee-ster oo ker-'zah-koo]
    Put on your coat.

Exercise 11

Translate the following.
1 Gosto muito da vossa casa.
2 Este é o seu copo e aquele é o dele.
3 A tua filha é muito simpática.
4 As nossas férias começam em junho.
5 A minha mulher chega sempre atrasada.
6 Are these your suitcases?
7 My telephone is always out of order.
8 This is not mine.
9 I don't know their name.
10 Your *(pl)* house is very far.
11 Our daughter is arriving tomorrow.
12 His friend *(m) is* American.

Vocabulary

gosto de ['goh 'sh-too d*e*]	I like
copo ['koh-poo]	glass
filha ['feel-y*e*r]	daughter
simpática [see*n*-'pah-tee-k*e*r]	nice, charming
férias ['feh-ree-*e*rsh]	holidays
começam [koo-'meh-saw*n*]	they begin
junho ['zhoon-yoo]	June
mulher [mool-'yehr]	wife
chega ['shay-g*e*r]	arrives
atrasada [*e*r-tre*r*-'zah-d*e*r]	late (*f sing*)
avariado [*e*r-v*e*r-ree-'ah-doo]	out of order
não sei ['nah-oo*n* say]	I don't know
o nome [oo 'noh-me*r*]	the name
longe ['lo*n*-zh*e*]	far
amanhã [*e*r-'me*r*n-yah*n*]	tomorrow
amigo [*e*r-'mee-goo]	friend
americano [*e*r-m*e*-ree-'k*e*r-noo]	American (*m sing*)

16 Cardinal numbers

1	**um** (*m*), **uma** (*f*)	15	**quinze**
2	**dois** (*m*), **duas** (*f*)	16	**dezasseis**
3	**três**	17	**dezassete**
4	**quatro**	18	**dezoito**
5	**cinco**	19	**dezanove**
6	**seis**	20	**vinte**
7	**sete**	21	**vinte e um/uma**
8	**oito**	22	**vinte e dois/duas**
9	**nove**	23	**vinte e três**
10	**dez**	30	**trinta**
11	**onze**	40	**quarenta**
12	**doze**	50	**cinquenta**
13	**treze**	60	**sessenta**
14	**catorze**	70	**setenta**

80	oitenta	500	quinhentos/as
90	noventa	600	seiscentos/as
100	cem	700	setecentos/as
101	cento e um/uma	800	oitocentos/as
102	cento e dois/duas	900	novecentos/as
120	cento e vinte	1000	mil
125	cento e vinte e cinco	1100	mil e cem
200	duzentos *(m)*	1101	mil cento e um/uma
	duzentas *(f)*	2000	dois/duas mil
201	duzentos/as e um/uma	100,000	cem mil
300	trezentos/as	1,000,000	um milhão
400	quatrocentos/as	2,000,000	dois milhões

IMITATED PRONUNCIATION (§16): (1-10) oo*n*, 'oo-me*r*, 'do'ish, 'doo-e*r*sh; traysh; 'kwah-tro; 'see*n*-koo; 'say'ish; sett; 'oh'it-too; 'noh've; daysh. (10-20) o*n*ze; dohze; 'tray-z*e*; ke*r*-'tor-z*e*; 'keen-z*e*; d*e*-zer-'say'ish; de*r*-zer-'sett; de-'zoh'it-too; d*e*-zer-'noh'v*e*; 'vee*n*-t*e*. (30-50) 'tree*n*-ter; kwe*r*-'ren-ter, si*n*-'kwen-ter. (100, 200, 1000, 1,000,000) se*n*; doo-'ze*n*-toosh; meel; meel'yah-oo*n*.

Note that when 100 is used as a noun, it is **a centena**. When 1000 is used as a noun, it is **um milhar**. Here are a few examples of numbers in use:

Já te disse centenas de vezes.
I have told you hundreds of times.
Estamos em mil novecentos e noventa e seis.
We are in 1996.
Quero três selos; um de vinte e cinco escudos, e dois de sessenta e cinco escudos.
I would like to have three stamps; one of 25 escudos and two of 65 escudos.
O meu pai faz hoje sessenta anos.
My father is sixty years old today. (*lit* He makes 60 years today.)
(Note the idiomatic use of the verb **fazer**.)

Os nossos amigos chegam no dia vinte e oito de maio.
Our friends arrive (will arrive) on the 28th of May.
(Note that the date is expressed by a cardinal number ('twenty eight') rather than an ordinal as in English 'twenty eighth'.)

Há dois meses que não como carne.
I have not eaten meat for two months.
(Note idiomatic use of **há** - see section 6.)

16a Ordinal numbers

primeiro/a	1st
segundo/a	2nd
terceiro/a	3rd
quarto/a	4th
quinto/a	5th
sexto/a	6th
sétimo/a	7th
oitavo/a	8th
nono/a	9th
décimo/a	10th
décimo primeiro/a	11th
décimo segundo/a	12th
etc	

vigésimo/a	20th
trigésimo/a	30th
quadragésimo/a	40th
quinquagésimo/a	50th
sexagésimo/a	60th
septuagésimo/a	70th
octogésimo/a	80th
nonagésimo/a	90th
centésimo/a	100th
milésimo/a	1000th
milionésimo/a	1,000,000th

17 Time/horas

Que horas são? What time is it?

São onze horas em ponto. It is 11 o'clock precisely.

São cinco e dez minutos. It is ten past five.

São oito e meia. It is half past eight.

São duas e vinte e cinco. It is twenty-five past two.

São quatro e um quarto. It is a quarter past four.

São vinte para as seis. It is twenty to six.

Faltam vinte para as seis. *A colloquial expression, literally* 'twenty missing out of six'.

São seis menos vinte. *Literally* 'six less twenty'.

São cinco e quarenta. *Literally* 'five and forty'.

É uma hora. It is one o'clock.

É meio dia. It is midday.

É meia noite. It is midnight.

Exercise 12

Translate the following:

1 Acabo o trabalho às seis horas.
2 Vamos passar quinze dias na praia.
3 Ela tem quatro irmãos.
4 O livro custa mil e duzentos escudos.
5 Este elevador leva só cinco pessoas.
6 Vou a Paris de quatro em quatro semanas.
7 Faço anos no dia 20 de setembro.
8 He begins his work at 8 o'clock.
9 She has two boys and three girls.
10 I write to my mother every five days.
11 He leaves on the 20th of May.
12 He has not worked for ten days.
13 I am thirty-five years old.
14 It is a quarter to six.

Vocabulary

acabo [er-'kah-boo]	I finish
passar [per-'sahr]	to spend
custa ['koosh-ter]	costs
elevador [ill-ver-'dor]	lift, elevator
leva ['leh-ver]	it takes, carries
só [soh]	only
pessoas [per-'soh-ersh]	people
Paris [per-'reesh]	Paris
de quatro em quatro semanas [se-'mer-nersh]	every four weeks
faço anos ['fah-soo 'er-noosh]	my birthday is
começa [koo-'meh-ser]	he/she begins
escrevo [ish-'kre-voo]	I write
mãe [mah'en]	mother
trabalha [trer-'bahl-yer]	he/she works

PRACTISE!

Study the following piece and its vocabulary list, then answer the questions in the exercise.

NO BANCO

Sr. Jones	Bom dia!
Empregado	Muito bom dia. Faz favor!
Sr. Jones	Queria abrir uma conta, por favor.
Empregado	Muito bem. Conta a prazo ou à ordem.
Sr. Jones	Queria uma à ordem agora e mais tarde a prazo.
Empregado	A taxa de juros agora está muito boa . . .
Sr. Jones	Sim?
Empregado	O senhor é residente em Portugal?
Sr. Jones	Sim, decidi viver neste lindo país de que gosto muito.
Empregado	Ainda bem! Faça o favor de preencher este impresso com o seu nome e morada nesta cidade e a sua última na Inglaterra; o nome do seu banco naquele país e o número da sua conta lá para obtermos referências. E, finalmente, a sua assinatura aqui em baixo.
Sr. Jones	Aqui está o impresso com todos os pormenores e devidamente assinado. Preciso de dinheiro. Posso trocar as minhas libras aqui ou tenho de ir para aquela fila?
Empregado	Não, pode trocar aqui.
Sr. Jones	A como está o câmbio da libra esterlina?
Empregado	A libra hoje está muito boa. Está a duzentos e quarenta escudos. Aqui tem a sua ficha, número 41. Faça o favor de ir ali à Caixa 3 e esperar que chamem o seu número para receber o dinheiro.

queria	I would like *(queria = the imperfect tense of querer to want, often used in place of the conditional)*
muito bem	very well
a prazo	deposit account
à ordem	current account *(in Brazil:* **conta corrente** *(f)*
mais tarde	later (on)
Sim?	Yes? (Really?)
a taxa de juros	the interest rate
muito boa	very good *(f)*
decidi	I decided
viver	to live
país	country
de que gosto muito	that I like so much
Ainda bem!	So glad! *(idiomatic expression which also means* 'thank goodness' *and, by changing intonation,* 'just as well')
prencher este impresso	to fill in this form
última	last (one)
lá	there (over there)
para obtermos	so that we get
finalmente	finally
assinatura	signature
aqui em baixo	down here (at the bottom)
todos os pormenores	all the details
devidamente assinado	duly signed
preciso de dinheiro	I need money
posso trocar as minhas libras?	can (may) I exchange my pounds?
ou	or
ir	to go
fila	queue
a como está o câmbio?	what (how much) is the rate of exchange?
ficha	*here: a numbered chip or* token
número	number
caixa	cash desk/window
esperar	to wait
que chamem	that they call
receber	to receive

Exercise P.4

See how well you can recall the dialogue at the bank, by completing the following sentences. Check the text 'No Banco' to see which words you should have put in the spaces:

1 Queria ___ uma ___ .
2 Conta a ___ ou ___ ___ ?
3 A taxa de ___ agora ___ ___ ___ .
4 Sim, decidi ___ neste ___ ___ de que ___ ___ .
5 Faça o favor de ___ este ___ com o seu nome e ___ nesta
___ e a sua ___ na Inglaterra; o ___ do seu banco ___
país e o ___ da sua conta ___ para ___ ___ .
É, finalmente, a sua ___ aqui ___ ___ .
6 Aqui está o ___ com ___ ___ ___ e devidamente ___ .
___ de dinheiro. Posso ___ as minhas libras ___ ou
___ ___ ___ para ___ ___ ?
7 A ___ está o câmbio da ___ ___ ?
8 A libra hoje está ___ ___ . Aqui ___ a sua ___ , número 41.
Faça o favor ___ ___ ali à ___ 3 e esparar que ___ o seu
___ para ___ o dinheiro.

18 Days of the week/dias da semana

domingo [doo-'meen-goo] Sunday
segunda-feira [se-'goon-der 'fay-rer] Monday
terça-feira ['tayr-ser fay-rer] Tuesday
quarta-feira ['kwahr-ter] Wednesday
quinta-feira ['keen-ter] Thursday
sexta-feira ['saysh-ter] Friday
sábado ['sah-ber-doo] Saturday

Hoje é domingo. Today is Sunday.
Amanhã será segunda-feira. Tomorrow will be Monday.
Depois de amanhã será terça-feira. The day after tomorrow will be Tuesday.

Ontem foi sábado. Yesterday was Saturday.
Anteontem *(also:* **antes de ontem) foi sexta-feira.** The day before yesterday was Friday.
hoje à noite tonight
esta tarde this afternoon
esta manhã this morning
amanhã de manhã tomorrow morning
amanhã à noite tomorrow evening/night
daqui a quinze dias in a fortnight's time
na próxima semana next week *(also:* **na semana que vem)**
no mês passado last month
véspera the day before

19 Months of the year/meses do ano

janeiro [zher-'nare-roo] January
fevereiro [fev-'rare-roo] February
março ['mahr-soo] March
abril [er-'breel] April
maio ['mah-yoo] May
junho ['zhoon-yoo] June
julho ['zhool-yoo] July
agosto [er-'goh'stoo] August
setembro [se-'ten-broo] September
outubro [oh-'too-broo] October
novembro [noo-'ven-broo] November
dezembro [de-'zen-broo] December

20 Seasons of the year, good wishes

a primavera [er pree-mer-'veh-rer] spring
o verão [oo ve-'rah'oon], **o estio** [oo ersh-'tee-oo] summer
o outono [oo oh-'toh-noo] autumn
o inverno [oo een-'vehr-noo] winter

a **Consoada** Christmas Eve
o **Natal** Christmas
Feliz Natal Happy Christmas
a **Véspera do Ano Novo** New Year's Eve
Ano Novo New Year
Ano Novo muito próspero Prosperous New Year
a **Quaresma** Lent
a **Páscoa** Easter
Páscoa feliz Happy Easter
Parabéns Happy Birthday (*also:* congratulations at a
    wedding, birth, etc.)
Boa sorte Good luck
Felicidades Much happiness (*also:* Many Happy Returns)
Feliz aniversário Happy anniversary

Exercise 13

Translate the following:

1 Na próxima semana vou a casa da minha tia.
2 No mês passado o meu irmão foi para o Brasil
    trabalhar.
3 Os meus filhos chegam daqui a quinze dias.
4 Hoje à noite vamos ao teatro.
5 A primavera é a minha estação favorita.
6 Ontem esteve muito frio.
7 Depois de amanhã temos os resultados dos nossos
    exames.
8 I am going to spend Christmas with my friends in
    Lisbon.
9 This year I have no holidays.
10 She is going to spend summer in the Algarve.
11 Yesterday was hot.
12 My birthday is on Sunday.
13 Tomorrow morning I begin work.
14 July, August and September are very hot months in
    Portugal.

Vocabulary

foi [foh'*e*]	went
vamos ['ve*r*-moosh]	we are going
esteve [ish-'tay-v*e*]	was
fez [faysh]	made/did
passar [pe*r*-'sahr]	to spend time
férias ['feh-re-e*r*sh]	holidays
faço ['fah-soo]	I do/make
começo [koo-'meh-soo]	I begin
meses muito quentes ['may-z*e*sh 'mwee*n*-too 'ke*n*-te*s*h]	very hot months

CONVERSATIONS

The time and weather

1

A   Desculpe. Dizia-me por favor que horas são?

B   Desculpe, mas não lhe posso dizer as horas, porque o meu relógio está parado. Mas, oiça – parece-me que o relógio da catedral está a dar horas.

A   Tem razão. Está, na verdade, a dar horas. São três horas.

2

A   Estou muito preocupada.

B   Então porquê?

A   Já são seis e vinte e o meu marido ainda não chegou. Está sempre atrasado.

B   Não estou de acordo. No meu relógio tenho seis e um quarto. O seu relógio deve estar adiantado.

A   Não pode ser; o meu relógio está sempre certo. Além disso ouvi, ainda há pouco, as notícias das dezóito horas (18.00).

B   Nesse caso é o meu que não está a trabalhar bem. Mas, quanto ao seu marido, – não se esqueça que é a hora de ponta* e que é sexta-feira.

A   Já se faz tarde para o teatro. Há que tempos que eu ando a tentar arranjar bilhetes. Finalmente consegui. Mas, esta noite o espectáculo começa às sete e quinze.

B   Ainda tem tempo. Olhe, aqui vem o seu marido.

A   Ainda bem!

*In Brazil: a hora do rush'

3

A Você acha que faz calor de mais no Algarve em junho?

B Não. Creio que ainda é suportável, e as praias não têm tanta gente como nos outros meses do verão. Eu confesso que prefiro ir para o sul da Europa no outono. Não aguento o calor. E em outubro e novembro ainda há muito sol em Portugal mas não faz tanto calor.

A Eu só posso ter férias em junho; e além disso dou--me muito bem com o calor. Detesto a chuva, o vento e o frio.

B Eu também.

TRANSLATION

1

A Excuse me. Would you please tell me what time it is?

B I am sorry, but I cannot tell you the time because my watch has stopped. But listen – I believe that (*literally* it seems to me that) the cathedral clock is striking.

A You are right. It is indeed striking. It is three o'clock.

2

A I am very worried.

B Yes, why?

A It is already twenty past six and my husband has not arrived yet. He is always late.

B   I do not agree. My watch says (*literally* on my watch I have) a quarter past six. Your watch must be fast.

A   It can't be. My watch is always right. Besides, I heard the six o'clock news on the radio a while ago.

B   In that case, it is mine that is not working (well). But, about your husband – don't forget it's the rush hour and that it's Friday.

A   It's getting late for the theatre. I have been trying to get tickets for ages. Finally I got them (*literally* I succeeded). But tonight the show starts at 7.15.

B   You still have time. Look – here comes your husband.

A   Just as well! (Thank goodness!)

3

A   Do you think it is too hot in the Algarve in June?

B   No. I believe that it is still bearable, and the beaches do not have as many people as in the other summer months. I must say (I confess) I prefer to go to the south of Europe in the autumn. I cannot bear the heat. And in October and November it is still very sunny in Portugal (*literally* there is still much sun), but it is not so hot (*literally* it does not do so much heat).

A   I can only have (my) holidays in June; and besides I like (*literally* I get on with) the heat. I hate the rain, wind and cold.

B   Me too. (So do I.)

Please repeat the following expressions:

1

dizia-me [dee-'zee'er-me] would you tell me?/did you tell me?/were you telling me? *(This is the imperfect tense of the verb **dizer** [dee-'zayr] to say, to tell. In Portuguese this tense is often used instead of the conditional.)*

oiça ['oh'e-ser] listen/hear *(imperative form of the verb **ouvir** to hear)*

parece-me [per-'reh-se-me] it seems to me, it appears

dar horas [dahr 'oh-rersh] to strike the hour *(literally to give hours)*

na verdade [ner ver-'dah-de] indeed, in fact, in truth

2

estou muito preocupada [pry'oh-koo-'pah-der] I am very worried

ainda não chegou ['she-go] not yet arrived

estou de acordo [ish-'toh der-'kohr-doo] I agree

não pode ser it cannot be

além disso [ah-'len 'dee-soo] besides that, besides

ainda há pouco [er-'een-der ah 'po-koo] a while ago

nesse caso [''eh-se 'kah-zoo] in that case

quanto a as to, as for, regarding, speaking of

não se esqueça ['nah'oon s'ish-'keh-ser] do not forget

hora de ponta/hora de movimento ['pon-ter/moo-vee-'men-too] rush hour

já se faz tarde [zhah se fahsh 'tar-de] it is becoming late

há que tempos [ah ke 'ten-posh] for ages

ando a tentar I have been trying *(present of verb **andar** to walk/to move/to be)*

ainda tem tempo you still have time, you are still in time

ainda bem thank goodness

3

não aguento [er-'gwen-too], **não suporto** [soo-'pohr-to] I can't bear, I can't stand

deu-me muito bem com ['do-me moo'in-too ben] I get on very well with/in

posso ['poss-soo] I can

eu também so do I

Other vocabulary

relógio [re-'loh-zhe'oo]	watch, clock
atrasado [er-trer-'zah-doo]	slow, late
adiantado [er-dy'an-'tah-doo]	fast
certo ['sehr-too]	right, correct
arranjar [er-'ran-jahr]	to get, obtain, arrange
bilhetes [bee-'yeh-tesh]	tickets
finalmente [fee-nahl-'men-te]	finally, at last
consegui *past tense of* **conseguir**	to succeed, to manage, to achieve, to be able to
espectáculo [ish-peh-'tah-koo-loo]	show
acha? ['ah-sher]	do you think?
gente* ['zhen-te]	people

(*Note that **gente** is singular in form and requires a singular verb although it is translated by an English plural, 'people'. For example: **a gente** *é* = the people *are*. Colloquially, **gente** + 3rd person singular of the verb has come to mean 'we'. Thus, **a gente é = nós somos.**)

From now on, there will not be a full translation of the conversational matter; only repetition and translation of new expressions and words. The imitated pronunciation will also be discontinued; if you are still having difficulty with this aspect of the language, our cassette recordings of the text will help considerably.

Chapter 5

The fifth chapter concentrates on feminine and plural forms of nouns and adjectives. Other topics include:

- *the past definite tense (simple past), in the three regular conjugations*
- *the command form (polite imperative), in both regular and irregular verbs*

21 The feminine forms of adjectives and nouns

As we have seen in chapter 1, nouns and adjectives are either masculine or feminine. We have learnt how to identify them and change from one gender to the other where applicable. For example:

o gato, a gata cat
o velho, a velha old man, old woman
António, Antónia
pintor, pintora painter
francês, francesa French
espanhol, espanhola Spanish
alemão, alemã German

And now that you have a clear picture, we add a little spice. There are nouns ending in **a** which are masculine. They are Greek derivatives mainly. For example:

o **tema** the theme
o **sistema** the system
o **clima** the climate
o **telefonema** the telephone call
o **quilograma** the kilo
o **panorama** the panorama, view
o **poeta** the poet
o **dia** the day
o **mapa** the map

But the noun **criança** ('child') is always preceded by the feminine article **(a criança)** and refers to both sexes.

Nouns and adjectives ending in **e**, in general do not alter; only the preceding article changes according to the gender:

o **estudante, a estudante** the student *m & f*
o **lápis verde** the green pencil
a **caneta verde** the green pen
um **quarto grande** a large bedroom
uma **sala grande** a large sitting-room

But **gente** (people) is always preceded by the feminine article, and is singular – as mentioned in the previous chapter.

Nouns and adjectives ending in **-ista** refer to both genders but their preceding article changes accordingly:

o **pianista, a pianista** male pianist, female pianist
o **artista, a artista** performer
o **telefonista, a telefonista** switchboard/telephone operator
o **vigarista, a vigarista** crook, swindler
comunista, fascista etc

Adjectives ending in a consonant generally remain unchanged:

um **homem agradável** a pleasant man;
uma **mulher agradável** a pleasant woman
o **rapaz está feliz** the boy is happy;
a **rapariga está feliz** the girl is happy
uma **lição simples** an easy lesson;
um **caso simples** a simple case

-eu usually changes to -eia. For example: **Europeu, Europeia**

Some nouns ending in -or usually change to -riz:

a(c)tor, a(c)triz actor, actress
embaixador, embaixatriz ambassador, ambassador's wife

Other nouns as well as additives have an 'a' added to the 'r'. For example:

embaixadora the lady ambassador
encantador, encantadora charming man, charming woman

Adjectives which end in -u (not -eu) form their feminine by adding **a**. For example:

cru, crua raw, uncooked
nu, nua naked, bare

As we have seen, nouns ending in -ao generally lose the -o in the feminine. In their irregular form they change to -ona (excepting **cão**, which see below):

comilão, comilona glutton, gluttonous
mandrião, mandriona lazy man/woman; lazy

comilão, comilona glutton, gluttonous
mandrião, mandriona lazy man/woman; lazy

Irregular adjectives:

mau, má	bad (*m & f*)
bom, boa	good (*m & f*)
dois, duas	two (*m & f*)

Also note the nouns **poeta** (*m* poet), **poetisa** (*f* poetess). In many cases the feminine is altogether different from its masculine counterpart. More examples: **cão, cadela** (dog, bitch), **pai, mãe** (father, mother), **avô, avó** (grandfather, grandmother), etc.

Exercise 14

Fill in the blanks:

1 Hoje o tempo está ___. (bad)
2 Ela é uma ___ ___ .(good secretary)
3 Não sei onde está ___ ___ ___ ___. (my French map)
4 ___ ___ (My sister) é mais ___ (old) do que eu.
5 ___ ___ ___ (My friend, *f*) é ___ (Spanish) mas o marido dela é ___. (English)
6 É uma ___ ___ (good thing) que você faz.
7 Há ___ ___ ___ (many pleasant people) neste mundo.
8 O meu colega está muito ___ (happy) no Brasil.
9 O Mercado Comum é uma comunidade ___. (European)
10 A mãe da minha amiga é ___ ___.(a poet)
11 Tenho um ___ ___ ___. (large green car)
12 Meu primo é um ___ ___ (good writer) e a mulher dele é também ___ ___ ___. (writer)
13 O António é um ___ ___. (Portuguese journalist)
14 Esta galinha está ___. (uncooked)

Vocabulary

tempo	weather
não sei	I don't know
coisa	thing
neste mundo	in this world
comunidade	community
jornalista	journalist
galinha	chicken
escritor	writer

22 Plural of nouns and adjectives

As seen in chapter 1, the general rule is to add an **s** to nouns and adjectives ending in a vowel in order to form the plural, and **es** to those that end in r, s, z. For example:

casa becomes **casas**
amante becomes **amantes** (lovers)
feliz becomes **felizes**
flor becomes **flores**
francês becomes **franceses**

Please note: nouns and adjectives ending in **-ês** lose their accent in the plural.

Nouns and adjectives ending in **-m** change **-m** to **-ns** in the plural. For example:

o homem becomes **os homens** (the man, the men)
a viagem becomes **as viagens** (the journey, the journeys)

Nouns and adjectives ending in **-al, -el, -ol, -ul** change **-l** to **-is** in the plural. For example:

a capital becomes **as capitais**
espanhol becomes **espanhóis**
o papel becomes **os papéis**
azul becomes **azuis** (blue)

When the noun ends in **-el** or **-ol** in the singular it will have an acute accent in the plural, for phonetic reasons. There's a change of sound, too, affecting a number of masculine words with 'o' in the last-but-one syllable; this letter has a closed sound in the singular but opens in the feminine and plural:

formoso [foor-'mor-soo], **formosa, formosos** [foor-'moh-ser, foor-'moh-soosh]

You will come across a few nouns and adjectives which end in **-s** in the singular; they will be the same in the plural:

um lápis   dois lápis
um caso simples   uns casos simples

Those ending in -il form their plural in two different ways, depending on whether the -il is stressed or not:
Stressed -il is changed to -is. E.g.: civil becomes civis
Unstressed -il is changed to -eis. E.g.: fácil becomes fáceis

Nouns and adjectives ending in -ão form the plural in one of three ways, as follows:

-ão to -oes
This is the most commonly-found method of changing -ao words into the plural. For example:

o limão lemon, becomes os limões
a lição lesson, becomes as lições
o leão lion, becomes os leões

-ão to -ães
The most commonly used nouns in this rule are:

o capitão captain, becomes os capitães
o alemão German, becomes os alemães
o cão dog, becomes os cães
o pão loaf of bread, becomes os pães

-ão to -ãos
There are very few examples of this type. The most important are the following:

o irmão brother, becomes os irmãos
a mão hand, becomes as mãos
o cristão Christian, becomes os cristãos
o órfão orphan, becomes os órfãos
o cidadão citizen, becomes os cidadãos

Note that in Portuguese, a masculine plural can include both sexes. For example, pais can mean 'fathers', but frequently means 'parents'. Similarly, filhos can mean 'sons' but also means 'children'. Tios can mean 'uncles' but also 'uncle and aunt', and so on.

Exercise 15

Translate the following:

1 Two sitting-rooms.
2 My brother and sister.
3 The flowers are beautiful.
4 These problems are difficult.
5 In the summer, there are many people on the beaches.
6 Three English students.
7 Four sheets.
8 My friends (*m &f*) are very kind.
9 I do not know these men.
10 The German children do not like the dogs.
11 I buy five loaves of bread every day.
12 She likes all animals.
13 My sister has blue eyes.
14 I have dirty hands.
15 (These lemons are good.
16 My parents are always so happy.

Vocabulary

sala /sala de estar	sitting room
linda	pretty, beautiful
problema	problem
praias	beaches
lençol	sheet
amável	kind
não conheço	I do not know
crianças (f)	children
todos	all
olhos	eyes
sujas	dirty
saúde	health
tão	so, as
gostar de	to like

23 The past definite

(also known as the preterite or simple past tense)

The past definite ('I spoke', I have spoken', 'I did speak') of the three regular conjugations is formed by adding the following terminations (shown in bold type) to the stem of the verb:

	falar (to speak)	**comer** (to eat)	**abrir** (to open)
eu	fal**ei**	com**i**	abr**i**
tu	fal**aste**	com**este**	abr**iste**
ele, ela, você	fal**ou**	com**eu**	abr**iu**
nós	fal**ámos**	com**emos**	abr**imos**
eles, vocês	fal**aram**	com**eram**	abr**iram**

Exercise 16

1 Ontem recebi uma carta da minha amiga.
2 Nós gostámos muito da sua casa.
3 Na semana passada visitámos uma escola muito moderna.
4 Eles partiram para o Brasil.
5 Vocês já venderam a vossa casa?
6 Não, ainda não vendemos a nossa casa.
7 Eles ainda não escreveram.
8 I did not understand.
9 What did they drink?
10 I have already eaten.
11 When did they leave?
12 At what time did the train leave?
13 We did not open the window.
14 He did not eat last night.
15 Did you (*informal*) speak to your mother?
16 I met (knew)* your brother in Lisbon.

88

Vocabulary

beber	to drink
já	already
a que horas	at what time
chegar	to arrive
janela	window
ontem à noite	last night
mãe	mother
conhecer*	to know
Lisboa	Lisbon

*The verb **conhecer** - to know - is used in Portuguese to express the English verb 'to meet' in situations where it means `to meet someone for the first time' - on being introduced, for example. In other situations, the verb 'to meet' is normally **encontrar**. See further explanation on page 101.

PRACTISE!

Problemas con telefones

*A Joana entra nos Correios para fazer uma chamada
telefónica.*

Joana	Faz favor! Quero fazer um telefonema.
Empregada	Cabine número três está livre. Faça favor!
Joana	Quanto custa uma chamada para o Norte?
Empregada	É o mesmo para todo o país. A sua chamada depende dos impulsos que gastar.

*Joana marca o número mas não consegue ligação. Ela
telefona às Reclamaçoes.*

Telefonista	Reclamações!
Joana	Ó minha senhora, não consigo obter sinal do número que desejo.
Reclamações	Não estará impedido?
Joana	Não, a linha parece estar morta.
Reclamações	Um momento que vou verificar. Não desligue. Qual ee o número que pretende?
Joana	54-0345.
Reclamações	Falta um algarismo. Depois do indicativo 54 tem que ter cinco algarismos. É melhor dirigir-se às informações através do número 118.
Informações	Informações!
Joana	Preciso de verificar o número do telefone de uma amiga minha.
Informações	Qual é o nome?
Joana	Rita Martim.
Informaçoes	Martins?
Joana	Não, Martim, sem 'S'.
Informações	Morada?
Joana	Rua do Torto, número dezasseis.
Informações	Rua do Porto, no. 16.
Joana (desperada)	Não, minha senhora . . . do Torto. 'T' como em tonta.
Informações	Pronto! Já compreendi. Não se aflija!

entra	goes in
correios	post, post-office
um telefonema, uma chamada telefónica	a phone call
empregada	clerk; employee
cabine	booth
é o mesmo	it's the same
o Norte	the North
impulsos que gastar	the units you spend
país	country
marca, *v* marcar	to dial
ligação	connection
consegue	she doesn't succeed (*verb* **conseguir**)
Reclamações!	Operator! (*lit* complaints)
telefonista	telephonist, operator
consigo	I'm (not) succeeding (*verb* **conseguir**)
obter	to obtain
que desejo	that I want/wish
sinal	tone; sign
não estará impedido?	it might be engaged
a linha parece estar morta	the line appears to be dead
vou verificar	I'm going to check
não desligue	don't ring off; don't put the phone down
que pretende	that you want
falta um algarismo	a digit is missing; you are short of a digit
depois do indicativo	after the code number
é melhor	it is better
dirigir-se às . . .	to contact the . . .
Informações	Enquiries
através de (o)	through, via
verificar	to check
pronto	O. K.
já compreendi	I have understood; I've got it
não se aflija	don't worry; don't get nervous

Exercise P. 5

Please answer the following questions. (As with Exercise P. 2, your answers should be checked by reference to the preceding diaologue):

1 Qual e o número da cabine que está livre?
2 Quanto custa uma chamada para o Norte?
3 De que depende o custo (the cost)?
4 Ela consegue fazer a ligação?
5 Repita o que Joana disse às Reclamações.
6 Não estará impedido?
7 Qual é o problema com o número da Joana?
8 Qual é o conselho (advice) que as Reclamações lhe dão?
9 De que precisa a Joana?
10 A amiga dela chama-se Martins?
11 Qual foi a resposta (reply, answer) mordaz (sharp) que Joana deu?
12 Que respondeu (replied) a telefonista?

24 Polite form of the imperative

This is in fact the subjunctive mood.

Regular verbs

	falar to speak	**comer** to eat	**abrir** to open
singular	Fal**e** Speak!	Com**a** Eat!	Abr**a** Open!
plural	Fal**em** Speak!	Com**am** Eat!	Abr**am** Open!
Let us …	Fal**emos**	Com**amos**	Abr**amos**

The true Portuguese imperative has in fact only two persons; **tu** (you *familiar*) and **vós** (you *pl formal*):

falar	**comer**	**abrir**
fala	come	abre
falai	comei	abri

In the negative form as well as in the polite form, the subjunctive mood is used as shown above. See the Appendix (verb table).

Irregular verbs

With certain exceptions *(see* Appendix), the polite imperative of irregular verbs is formed from the stem of the first person singular of the present indicative plus the endings shown in bold in the following table of common irregular verbs:

	ver to see	**trazer** to bring	**fazer** to do/make	**dar** to give
singular	Veja	Traga	Faça	Dê
plural	Vejam	Tragam	Façam	Dêem
Let us . . .	Vejamos	Tragamos	Façamos	Dêmos

	dizer to say	**ser** to be	**estar** to be	**querer** to want
singular	Diga	Seja	Esteja	Queira
plural	Digam	Sejam	Estejam	Queiram
Let us . . .	Digamos	Sejamos	Estejamos	

	ter to have	**vir** to come	**ir** to go	**pôr** to put
singular	Tenha	Venha	Vá	Ponha
plural	Tenham	Venham	Vao	Ponham
Let us . . .	Tenhamos	Venhamos	Vamos	Ponhamos

As you will have deduced(from the table of regular verbson the preceding page), **vega, vejam, traga, tragam** etc mean 'see!', 'bring!' and so on.

Exercise 17

1 Venha cá.
2 Fale devagar.
3 Não faça barulho.
4 Vá por ali.
5 Não seja tonto.
6 Esteja quieto.
7 Traga a lista dos vinhos.
8 Speak slowly.
9 Let us open the window.
10 Shut *(pl)* the door.
11 Do not eat *(pl) so* quickly.
12 Let us see . . .
13 Come *(pl)* at once.
14 Let us go.
15 Do not speak *(pl)* so loudly.
16 Don't say anything.

Vocabulary

cá	here
devagar	slowly
barulho	noise
por ali	that way, over there
tonto	silly
quieto	still
lista de vinhos	wine list
fechar	to close
tão depressa	as quickly
já	already, at once, straight away
nada	nothing, anything
ali	there
por ali	over there, that way, through there
alto	loud, loudly, high, tall

24a Other translations of 'to be'

Apart from **ser/estar** there are other ways of saying 'to be' in Portuguese. One example is **andar,** an auxiliary verb which means 'to be', 'to go', 'to walk'. This requires some explanation. You must think of it as the verb of 'movement' not only in respect of space but also of time, so, when it is used instead of **estar** its present tense is best translated in English by a perfect tense. For example:

ando a tentar I have been trying
    (the idea is over a certain period)
ela anda grávida (also: **está grávida)**

It is used in all types of transport (movement), as follows:

andar a pé	to walk
andar a cavalo	to ride/go on horseback
andar de aviao	to fly
andar de barco	to go by boat
andar de comboio	to go by train
andar de carro	to drive/go by car

Ficar is another auxiliary verb which means 'to be' but which is employed in a different way. It also means 'to stay', 'to remain'. Use it for location:

Onde fica o Centro de Turismo?
    Where is the Tourist Office?
(In this case you could equally well use either **estar or ser.**)

Ficar is preferred to **estar** in expressions of emotion resulting from some news:

Fiquei tão contente ao ler a tua carta.
    I was (became) so pleased/happy when I read your letter.

Note also:

Fico à espera de tua resposta.
    I await (remain waiting for) your reply.
Vou ficar naquela casa.
    I am going to stay in that house.

ficar com	to keep, to have
fico com as chaves	I'll keep the keys
fico com este	I'll have this one
ficar bem/mal	to suit/not to suit
Esta cor fica-lhe bem	This colour suits you

CONVERSATION

Um emprego em Moçambique/A job in Mozambique

Luisa A sua irmã Ann sempre conseguiu o tal emprego em Moçambique?

Jane Sim, recebeu a resposta há duas semanas, depois de muitas entrevistas e de esperar seis meses. Está nas suas sete quintas, porque já desesperava de ser aceite. O ordenado é bom, mas o que mais lhe agrada é a oportunidade de conhecer um país do 'terceiro mundo'.

Luisa Que género de trabalho é? Não me lembro do que ela me disse.

Jane Ela vai ensinar matemática numa escola secundária. Aparentemente há lá falta de professores. Já está tudo arranjado. Só falta o visto. Você sabe que ela vai primeiro a Lisboa por dois meses em curso de férias, com todas as despesas pagas?

Luisa Não, não sabia nada disto. Que bom! E que sorte!

Jane É verdade. Tanto mais que o noivo também tem esperanças de ir para lá. Precisam de engenheiros civis. Ele respondeu a um anúncio e agora está à espera de resposta. Tanto ele como a Ann querem conhecer a África.

Luisa Mas ele fala português?

Jane Fala sim, e fluentemente. Ele tirou um curso de português há anos, e depois esteve a trabalhar em Lisboa uns anos.

Luisa E quando se casam?

Jane Tencionam casar-se daqui a dois anos se tudo correr bem.

Luisa Quando parte a Ann para Lisboa?

Jane Na próxima quinta-feira, no voo da TAP. Oxalá não haja nevoeiro ou greves.

Luisa *Vou* telefonar-lhe esta noite a desejar-lhe boa sorte. Adeus, até à vista.

Vocabulary

tal	such, that, the said . . .
receber	to receive
conseguir	to get, to obtain
conseguir + infinitive =	to manage to . . . , to succeed in . . .
sempre	always, after all, in the end, finally
sempre conseguiu	*(idiomatic use of sempre)* she obtained in the end
responder	to reply
resposta	an answer, a reply
há duas semanas	two weeks ago
há anos	years ago *(see idiomatic uses of* haver *in section 6*
depois de	after
entrevista	interview
quinta	farm
Está nas suas sete quintas.	*(idiomatic expression)* She is in her seventh heaven/ over the moon. *(lit.* She is in her seven farms.)
desesperar de	to despair, to give up hope of
aceitar	to accept
ser aceite	to be accepted
ordenado	salary
agradar	to please
o que mais lhe agrada . . .	what pleases her most . . .
terceiro mundo	third world
género	type, kind
lembrar-se de	to remember
ensinar	to teach
escola secundária	secondary school
faltar	to be lacking, to be missing
falta	shortage
Há lá falta.	There is a shortage over there.
arranjar	to arrange, to get

Já está tudo arranjado.	Everything is already arranged.
visto	visa
curso de férias	summer (holiday) course
despesas	expenses
todas as despesas pagas	all expenses paid
saber	to know
Não sabia nada disto.	I didn't know anything about it.
Que bom!	How marvellous!
verdade	truth
É verdade.	That's right. That's so.
tanto mais	besides, moreover, particularly as
noivo	fiancé, bridegroom
noiva	fiancée, bride
esperança	hope
precisar de	to need
engenheiros civis	civil engineers
anúncio	advertisement
Tanto ele como a Ann . . .	Both he and Ann . . .
uns anos	a few years, for a few years *(see uses of indef. art. in section 3)*
tencionar + *infinitive*	to intend to
casar-se	to marry, to get married
daqui a dois anos	in two years from now
correr	to go, to proceed, to run
se tudo correr bem	if all goes well
voo	flight
Oxalá . . . Oxalá não . . .	I do hope. . I hope not . . . *This idiomatic expression derives from the Arabic* Insh' Allah, *meaning 'God willing'.*
nevoeiro	fog
greve	strike
desejar	to wish
Adeus	Goodbye
Até à vista.	'Bye for now, see you, *etc*

Chapter 6

A long section on the direct and indirect object forms of personal pronouns, and also the reflexive form, is the central topic in this unit. It also covers:

- the imperfect or past continuous tense
- some mealtime vocabulary
- adverbs of place
- letters (opening and closing formulae)

25 The imperfect tense

Sometimes called the past continuous, this is the tense used to express what was happening or used to happen in the past – <u>during</u> the past. In the *imperfect* the action is *incomplete* or *interrupted*, unlike the past definite. It is also the tense of description in the past. It is one of the easiest tenses to conjugate, since all verbs (regular and irregular) will have the same ending, depending on which of two groups they belong to. The first group consists of all verbs ending in -ar. In this, the imperfect tense ends in **-ava** etc. In the second group (verbs ending in **-er** and **-ir**) the imperfect ends in **-ia** etc.

	falar (to speak)	**comer** (to eat)	**abrir** (to open)
eu	fal**ava**	com**ia**	abr**ia**
tu	fal**avas**	com**ias**	abr**ias**
você	fal**ava**	com**ia**	abr**ia**
ele, ela	fal**ava**	com**ia**	abr**ia**
nós	fal**ávamos**	com**íamos**	abr**íamos**

vocês	fal**avam**	com**iam**	abr**iam**
eles, elas	fal**avam**	com**iam**	abr**iam**

There are only four exceptions in the second group:
ter (to have) **tinha, tinhas, tinha, tínhamos, tinham**
vir (to come) **vinha, vinhas, vinha, vínhamos, vinham**
pôr (to put) **punha, punhas, punha, púnhamos, punham**
ser (to be) **era, eras, era, éramos, eram**

The imperfect is frequently used in place of the conditional. For example, 'I would like to have . . . ' is expressed by **gostava de ter . . .** instead of **gostaria** (see also section 32).

Sentences illustrating the imperfect tense:

Era uma vez . . .
    Once upon a time . . .

'I did not know that . . . ' or 'I did not know whether . . . ' is rendered in the imperfect: **Não sabia que . . .** or **Não sabia se . . .** :

Não sabia* se vinham.
    I did not know whether they were coming.

Estava ao telefone quando ele entrou.
    I was on the phone when he came in.
('He came in' is the past definite as his action is complete; mine, on the other hand, was interrupted.)

Quando era pequena, brincava** com as tuas bonecas.
    When I was a child I played (used to play) with your dolls.

Ela jogava ténis todas as manhãs.
    She played tennis every morning. (habitual action)

Conhecia-os* bem há muito tempo.
    I used to know them well a long time ago.

But notice the past definite:

Conheci-os o ano passado. I met them last year.
(See section 23.)

Ela nunca comia bolos. She never used to eat cakes.

But:

Ela nunca comeu bolos. She has never eaten cakes.

* **Conhecer** to know (= to be acquainted with) can also be translated by 'to meet' (= for the first time), and **soube** – the past definite of **saber** to know (= knowledge) – is often translated by 'I heard' or 'I learnt'. In English we say `Can you swim?' but in Portuguese **Sabe nadar?** (= 'do you know how to swim?'); if you were to say **Pode?** ('can you?') it would imply that you had permission to do so, for **Não posso nadar** means 'I am not allowed to swim' (or that I cannot, due to some physical condition). It does not necessarily mean that I don't know how to swim.

** 'To play' can be translated in a variety of ways in Portuguese, depending on the context. In the example just seen, it means 'to play with toys'; the same verb, **brincar,** is also used when you want to talk about playing with children, or teasing. **Jogar** is the verb to use for playing games or sports, while **tocar** means 'to play music' or to ring a doorbell. (Coupled with the preposition **em, tocar** means 'to touch'.) **Desempenhar (um papel)** means 'to play (a role)'. Some examples follow; consult the dictionary for other translations of 'to play'.

Ela brinca no jardim.
    She is playing in the garden.
Não ligues nenhuma, ele está a brincar contigo.
    Don't pay any attention, he is teasing you.
Jogo as cartas.
    I play cards.
Ela toca guitarra.
    She plays the guitar.
O actor desempenhou o papel de Otelo muito bem.
    The actor played the part of Othello very well.

Exercise 18

Translate the following
1 Quando era criança aprendia tudo mais facilmente.
2 Eu antes comia muito, mas agora não.
3 Íamos todos os dias à praia.
4 Ontem fomos ao campo.
5 Era debaixo desta árvore que eu costumava sentar-me.
6 Que estava você a fazer?
7 Eu estava a tomar banho.
8 What time did you take your breakfast?
9 Would you please tell me where the bus-stop is?
10 I learned that your brother was going to Africa. Is it true?
11 It was raining cats and dogs when we went out.
12 He was listening while I was speaking.
13 I was already eating.
14 Last night I had dinner (dined) with my mother-in-law.

Vocabulary

aprender	to learn
tudo	everything
facilmente	easily
antes	before
agora não	not now
fomos	we went (*past definite of the verb* ir)
campo	country, countryside, (*also* a field)
debaixo	under, underneath
costumava	I used to, I was in the habit of
sentar-se	to sit down
a tomar banho	to take a bath
paragem do autocarro	bus-stop
É verdade?	Is it true?
chover	to rain
a cântaros	(raining) 'cats and dogs'
enquanto	while
sair	to go out
ouvir	to listen
sogra	mother-in-law

Translations of 'take'

- **tomar**   to take (i.e. ingest) food, drinks; to touch, seize, grasp (with your hands);
    to take (i.e. go by) a bus, train; to take a bath.

Eu tomo o autocarro *(Brazil:* **ônibus) às 9 horas.**
    I take the bus at 9 o'clock.

- **levar**   to take (in the sense of carrying); to take (in relation to time);
    idiom to charge (money).

Levo estas malas comigo.
    I take these suitcases with me.

O avião leva duas horas daqui para Lisboa.
    The plane takes two hours from here to Lisbon.

Quanto me leva você por isto?
    How much will you charge me for this?

- **tirar**   to take away, out, from; to take off, remove;
    to take photos, a course, an exam, a copy.

Ele tirou o casaco.
    He took his coat off.

Ela tirou-me a escova do cabelo.
    She took my hairbrush away.

Você tira muito boas fotografias.
    You take very good photos.

But:

O avião levanta voo *(Brazil:* **vôo).**
    The plane takes off.

- **levar** (to take), **trazer** (to bring), **ir** (to go), **vir** (to bring):
You are likely to feel confused about 'coming' and 'going'. Remember that **levar** and **ir** (*lit.* to take, to go) refer to the place away from the speaker and <u>not</u> to the person you are addressing, while **trazer** and **vir** (lit. to bring, to come) refer to the speaker. Thus, it is not 'I am coming to your house to bring flowers' but '**vou** (I'm going) **a sua casa para levar** (to take) **flores**'.

26 Meals/ Refeições

o pequeno-almoço breakfast *(in Brazil:* **café da manhã)**
o almoço lunch
o lanche tea-time; *also* **a merenda**
o jantar dinner
a ceia supper

and their respective verbs:

tomar o pequeno-almoço to take breakfast
almoçar to take lunch
lanchar to take mid-afternoon tea
jantar to dine

PRACTISE!

Um dia de anos/A birthday

Antónia O domingo passado foi o dia dos anos do meu sogro. Foi uma grande festa. Estava lá, praticamente, toda a família: os sobrinhos americanos do meu sogro, a tia do meu marido que veio do Brasil, os meus cunhados e cunhadas e os netos todos dos meus sogros que, ao todo, são nove.

Beatriz Meu Deus, tanta gente! Deve ter sido um pandemónio com essa malta toda.

Antónia Não, nem por isso. Estava tudo muito bem organizado. Como estava calor, mandámos os mais novos para a piscina e pusemos a gente mais velha a jogar xadrez. Nós, as mulheres, estávamos encarregadas de todos os preparativos, enquanto os maridos bebiam e discutiam os últimos acontecimentos.

Beatriz Quantos anos fez o seu sogro?

Antónia Fez sessenta e cinco anos.

Beatriz Não parece, está muito bem conservado. Quando o vir, dê-lhe os meus sinceros parabéns. Tem graça que a minha enteada também fez anos no dia vinte e oito. Fez dezoito anos. Mas com essa não tivemos problema. Ela foi para a discoteca com os amigos e nós só pagámos a conta. Voltando ao assunto da sua festa, que comeram?

Antónia Bem, para o almoço tivemos saladas, ovos, queijo, camarões, azeitonas e fruta – muitas uvas e melões e também melancia. Depois da sesta lanchámos: chá, torradas, biscoitos feitos em casa e o bolo dos anos com as velas. E por volta das oito jantámos. Era leitão assado no espeto – no jardim, é claro – ervilhas batatas e outros legumes. Para sobremesa tivemos uma grande variedade de pudins. O vinho era do melhor, das adegas do meu cunhado e, naturalmente, não faltava o champagne.

dia dos anos birthday
uma grande festa a great party
ao todo in all
tanta gente so many people
deve ter sido it must have been
com essa malta toda with all that crowd *(colloquial)*
nem por isso not really, not too bad
quantos anos fez . . . how old was . . .
não parece he does not look it, he does not appear . . .
bem conservado well preserved
quando o vir when you see him
parabéns happy birthday *(also* congratulations)
tem graça how funny, it is funny, what a coincidence
mas com essa with that one, with her
voltando ao assunto coming back to the subject
e por volta das oito and around eight o'clock
era do melhor it was of the best
não faltava we were not short of, there was no lack of
sogro/sogra father-in-law / mother-in-law
praticamente practically
toda a família the whole family
sobrinhos/ sobrinhas nephews / nieces
cunhados/cunhadas brothers-in-law / sisters-in-law
netos grandchildren
pandemónio pandemonium *(in Brazil:* **pandemônio)**
organizado organized *(the past participle of verb* **organizar)**
mandámos *past tense of* **mandar** to send, to order, to
    command
os mais novos the younger ones
pusemos *past tense of verb* **pôr** to put, to set *(irregular)*
mais velha older
xadrez chess
estávamos encarregadas we were in charge
enquanto while
os maridos the husbands
discutir to discuss
últimos acontecimentos the latest events
fazer to make, to do
Quantos anos fez? How old were you, was he/she?
dê-lhe give him *(imperative of* **dar)**
enteada stepdaughter

tivemos *past tense of verb* **ter**
foi went/ was
pagar to pay
ovos eggs
queijo cheese
camarões prawns (*also* shrimps)
azeitonas olives
uvas grapes
melões melons
melancia water melon
sesta nap (afternoon nap)
chá tea
torradas toast
biscoitos biscuits
feitos em casa made at home (*verb* **fazer**)
velas candles
leitão suckling pig
assado roasted
espeto spit
jardim garden
é claro of course, naturally
ervilhas peas
batatas potatoes
outros others
legumes vegetables
sobremesa dessert
variedade variety
pudins puddings (*sing.* **pudim**)
vinho wine
adegas wine cellars

Exercise P. 6

Answer the questions. and check your answers by reference to the preceding dialogue:

1 Quem são as protagonistas deste diálogo?
2 De quem falam?
3 O que aconteceu (what happened) no domingo?
4 Havia pouca gente?
5 Descreva a família.
6 Que faziam os jovens?
7 Quantos anos fez o sogro?
8 Ele parece muito velho?
9 Quem mais fez anos no dia vinte e oito?
10 Ela teve uma grande festa?
11 Quem pagou a conta?
12 Descreva o que comeram na festa dos anos - ao almoço, lanche e jantar.

27 Adverbs of place 'here', 'there'

aqui, cá	here	(practically no difference between these two, but **cá** tends to be used more idiomatically)
ali	there	(you can see it)
lá	there	(you don't have to see it; it is also employed in a more idiomatic sense)
aí	there	(is close to the person you're speaking to; it can also mean 'somewhere there')
acolá	there	(further than **ali** - 'over there', 'yonder')

Observe the following examples:

Estou aqui há muito tempo.
   I have been here for a long time.
Cá estou a escrever-te . . .
   Here I am writing to you . . .
Venha cá! (also: **Venha aqui!**)
   Come here!

O meu irmão está ali.
>My brother is there. (Pointing to the place.)

Como estava o tempo lá?
>How was the weather there? (Speaking of a place away from both speakers.)

Lá vai ela!
>There she goes!

When telephoning or writing to a friend about the place where she/he is now:

Como está o tempo aí?
>How is the weather there?

Onde estão as minhas luvas?
>Where are my gloves?

(Your friend in the next room will reply:)

Estão aí.
>They are there.

Vejo uma águia acolá, naquela montanha.
>I see an eagle over there, on that mountain.

Please note: **aqui, ali, aí** and **lá**, often combined with prepositions, can be used in expressions of time:

Daqui a 15 dias.
>In two weeks' time.

Dali, ele foi para Macau.
>From there, he went to Macau.

Já lá vão cinco anos!
>Five years have gone by!

When speaking outside your interlocutor's door:

Você nunca mais sai daí?
>When are you coming out of there? (Are you ever going to come out of there?)

Exercise 18a

1 O avião levou 6 horas para chegar lá.
2 Hoje não quero brincar com as crianças; prefiro jogar xadrez.
3 Ele vem cá muitas vezes.
4 Ela foi para Nova Iorque e dali foi para o México.
5 Senhor doutor, quantos comprimidos (pills/tablets) tenho de tomar?
6 Tive de (I had to) tirar dinheiro da minha conta--depósito.
7 How is the weather there? (Speaking to someone on the phone)
8 Your gloves are there. (Somewhere)
9 The bus-stop is there.
10 Here I am!
11 I see a boat over there. (Further away)
12 Your keys are here.

28 Personal object pronouns - direct and indirect, the reflexive form

SINGULAR

	Direct object	*Indirect object*	*Reflexive*
1st person	**me** me	**me** to/for me	**me** myself
2nd pers. fam.	**te** you	**te** to/for you	**te** yourself
2nd form. (m)	**o** you	**lhe** to/for you	**se** yourself
2nd form. (f)	**a** you	**lhe** to/for you	**se** yourself
3rd pers. (m)	**o** him, it	**lhe** to/for him, it	**se** himself, itself
3rd pers. (f)	**a** her, it	**lhe** to/for her, it	**se** herself, itself

PLURAL

1st person	**nos** us	**nos** to/for us	**nos** our-selves
2nd pers. fam.	**vos** you	**vos** to/for you	**vos** your-selves
2nd form. (m)	**os** you	**lhes** to/for you	se your-selves
2nd form. (f)	**as** you	**lhes** to/for you	se your-selves
3rd pers. (m)	**os** them	**lhes** to/for them	se them-selves
3rd pers. (f)	**as** them	**lhes** to/for them	se them-selves

Note that in the 3rd person (and therefore in the 2nd person formal), the direct object **o, a, os, as,** is different from the indirect object **lhe, lhes,** and from the reflexive pronoun **se.** In all other cases, however, the object and reflexive pronouns share the same forms.

Combined forms

The direct object pronoun combines with the indirect object pronoun to give the following compounds. Note that the indirect object pronoun always comes first, but number and gender are determined by the direct object.

me		**mo, ma, mos, mas**
te		**to, ta, tos, tas**
lhe		**lho, lha, lhos, lhas**
	plus **o, a, os, as** gives	
nos		**no-lo, no-la, no-los, no-las**
vos		**vo-lo, vo-la, vo-los, vo-las**
lhes		**lho, lha, lhos, lhas**

In the 1st and 2nd persons plural, the **s** of **nos** and **vos** is omitted and replaced by a hyphen before another pronoun. However, the combined forms **no-lo** etc, and **vo-lo** etc, are seldom used in conversation. For example:

Dou-lhe a minha morada. I give my address to him.
Dou-lha. I give him/her/you it. [i. e. **morada** (*f*)]

Word order

In affirmative main sentences, the object pronouns follow the verb and are joined to it by a hyphen. But there are certain circumstances in which they precede the verb, as follows:

1 *In negative sentences*
Não o vejo. I don't see him/you (*m formal*)

2 *In questions*
Porque não nos fala? Why don't you (*formal*) speak to us?

3 *After some prepositions, conjunctions and adverbs*
Sempre me detestou. He/she/you (*formal*) always hated me.
Depois de lhe dar a receita . . . After giving him/her/you (*formal*) the prescription . . .
Antes que me esqueça . . . Before I forget . . .
Eles mal me falam. They hardly speak to me.

Note that the verb **esquecer-se** (to forget) is reflexive in Portuguese.

3rd person pronouns after verbs ending in **r**, **s** *and* **z**

When a verb ends in *r, s* or *z*, the last letter is dropped before the 3rd person pronouns **o, a, os, as**. The letter *l* is then prefixed to the pronoun which is joined to the verb by a hyphen. The affected verbal forms will then be stressed, with an acute accent over the letter *a* and a circumflex over *e* and *o*. The following examples illustrate this point:

Eu quero ver o António. I want to see Anthony.
Eu quero vê-lo. I want to see him.

Eu desejo comprar uvas. I want to buy grapes.
Eu desejo comprá-las. I want to buy them.

Ela faz cestos. She makes baskets.
Ela fá-los. She makes them.

Nós vemos a sua amiga muitas vezes.
  We often see your friend.
Nós vemo-la muitas vezes.
  We often see her.

3rd person pronouns after verbs ending in **m**, **ão** *and* **õe**

When the pronouns **o, a, os, as,** come immediately after a verb ending in *m, ão* or *õe*, the letter *n* is prefixed to the pronoun to give the forms **no, na, nos, nas,** which are then joined to the verb by a hyphen as shown in the following examples:

Eles dão lições ao ar livre. They give lessons in the open air.
Eles dão-nas ao ar livre. They give them in the open air.

Elas viram o irmão da Maria. They saw Maria's brother.
Elas viram-no. They saw him.

Ela põe a mesa. She sets the table.
Ela põe-na. She sets it.

Note that the rule governing the position of object pronouns in negative and interrogative sentences still applies. E. g.:

Elas não o viram. They didn't see him.
Ela a põe? Is she setting it?

Word order in Brazil

In Brazilian Portuguese, the personal object pronouns nearly always come before the verb. Therefore in Brazil, the word order in the above examples would be:

Eles as dão ao ar livre.
Elas o viram.
Ela a põe.

In Brazil, the reflexive pronoun also comes before the verb. For example:

Eu me sinto cansada. I *(f)* feel tired.
In Portugal: Eu sinto-me cansada.

Object pronouns after prepositions

The pronouns you have studied go together with verbs. The following forms – disjunctive pronouns – come after prepositions and, therefore, are employed in the case of 'verb + preposition' (such as **gostar de**):

SINGULAR

1st person	**mim** me
2nd person familiar	**ti** you
2nd person formal	**si*, você, o senhor, a senhora** you
3rd person	**ele** him, **ela** her

PLURAL

1st person	**nós** us
2nd person formal	**vós, vocês** *(more casual),* **os senhores, as senhoras** you
3rd person	**eles, elas** them

* In addition to its translation of 'you', **si** can also mean 'him/herself', 'themselves'. For example:

Ele fala de si para si. He is speaking to himself.

The following examples illustrate the use of the disjunctive pronouns after prepositions:

Este livro é para mim. This book is for me.
Ele gosta de ti. He likes you *(familiar).*
Gosto dela. I like her.
Eu paguei por ela. I paid for her.
Eu acredito em si. I believe you. I believe in you *(formal).*

These pronouns are especially useful for avoiding the ambiguities to which the combined forms frequently give rise. For this reason, the disjunctive forms are much more common in speech. For example:

Dei-lhes o lápis I gave them the pencil, *becomes*
Dei-o a eles *in preference to* **Dei-lho.**

com – *an exception*

The preposition **com** meaning 'with' combines with the disjunctive pronouns **mim, ti, si, nós** and **vós** to give the following special forms:

SINGULAR

com + mim = comigo   with me
com + ti = contigo   with you *(familiar)*
com + si = consigo   with you *(formal)*
                  Also: with himself/herself/oneself
But note: **com ele, com ela** with him, with her

PLURAL

com + nós = conosco with us
com + vós = convosco with you
But note: **com eles, com elas** with them(*m & f*)

Some adverbs and prepositions commonly followed by these pronouns:

atrás de behind
perto de near
longe de far from
em frente de in front of
em cima de on, on top of
por baixo de under, below
contra against
sem without
entre between, among
antes de before
depois de after

Exercise 19

Translate the following:

1 Dê-lhe os meus cumprimentos.
2 Ela telefonou-me ontem à noite.
3 Viu-o na semana passada.
4 Não as conheço bem.
5 Eles visitam-nos todos os anos.
6 Queremos vê-lo.
7 Vou ajudá-la.
8 Vocês ajudam-no muito.
9 Ele não quer as maçãs, mas eu vou dar-lhas.
10 Você mora perto de mim.
11 Não como sem você.
12 Venha comigo agora tomar um café e depois eu vou consigo ao cabeleireiro.
13 Os cães estão connosco, mas os gatos estão com elas.
14 Quem lho disse?

Vocabulary

dê (dar)	give
cumprimentos	regards (best regards)
telefonar	to telephone
viu *past definite of* **ver**	to see
conhecer	to know, to be acquainted with
visitar	to visit
querer	to want
ajudar	to help
depois	after, afterwards, then
cabeleireiro	hairdresser
cães	dogs *(see section 22)*
gatos	cats
disse *past definite of* **dizer**	to say, to tell

Omission of the 3rd person pronoun referring to 'things'

When the pronoun corresponds to an inanimate object or an
abstract idea and comes at the end of a phrase or sentence, it
is often omitted, as the following examples show.

Você viu o filme, 'E tudo o vento levou'? Have you seen the
film, 'Gone with the Wind'?
Sim, vi. Yes, I have seen it.

O senhor come carne? Do you eat meat?
Sim, como. Yes, I eat it.

Gosta de Portugal? Do you like Portugal?
Sim, gosto. Yes, I like it.

Vocês beberam o vinho? Did you drink the wine?
Sim, bebemos. Yes, we drank it.

Exercise 20

Translate the following:

1 Show us what you found.
2 Go and look for her.
3 Are these flowers for me?
4 Before I forget, I have to tell you *(pl)*.
5 He waited for us.
6 Come with me.
7 There are no secrets between us.
8 I am counting on you *(familiar)*.
9 He did not lend it to me.
10 They help him.
11 My mother did not ring me up.
12 I don't need him.
13 I called him but he did not hear me.
14 I saw them *(m)* last week.
15 He is going to see her.

Vocabulary

mostrar	to show
procurar	to look for (*in Brazil*: **buscar**)
esperar	to wait
segredos	secrets
contar com	to count on, to count with
emprestar	to lend
ajudar	to help
telefonar	to telephone, to ring up
precisar de	to need
chamar	to call
ouvir	to hear
vi	I saw (*past tense of verb* **ver**)

Chapter 7

You now progress to the future and conditional tenses, plus learning about:

- 'either . . . or', 'neither . . . nor'
- negatives such as 'nothing', 'never' and so forth
- other indefinite adjectives and pronouns ('certain', 'few', 'all', 'some' etc)
- comparison of adjectives and adverbs
- how to use 'já'

29 'ou . . . ou' either . . . or, 'nem . . . nem' neither . . . nor

Quem manda aqui, sou eu ou você? Who is in charge here (*literally* who gives orders,) is it me or you?

Nem eu nem a minha mulher nem os meus filhos gostamos de ar condicionado. Neither I nor my wife nor my children like air conditioning.

When 'neither' is on its own ('neither one nor the other'), it must be translated by **nem um/a nem outro/outra.**

From the two sentences above you should note two things: one is that the subject pronoun **eu** comes first when there are other subject pronouns (**Eu e a minha mulher** instead of the English 'My wife and I'); and the other is that in Portuguese you may repeat the word **nem** 'neither, nor' as many times as necessary.

nem and **nem mesmo** translate 'not even'. For example:

Nem quero sonhar uma coisa dessas.
    I don't even want to think of *(lit.* dream of) such a thing.
Nem mesmo se o senhor me pagasse.
    Not even if you paid me.

Nem is sometimes used in place of **não**. For example:

Nem me diga . . . You don't say . . . Don't tell me . . .
Nem por isso. Not really.

29a Other negatives

nada nothing
nunca never
jamais never
nunca . . . mais never again
nunca mais never again
já não no longer; any more
ainda não not yet
ninguém no-one
nenhum *(m)*, **nenhuma** *(f)*, **nenhuns** *(m pl)*, **nenhumas** *(f pl)*
    none, any

Não conheço ninguém aqui.
    I don't know anyone here.
Ele não tem nenhuma ideia.
    He hasn't any idea.
Nunca mais compro sapatos de salto alto.
    Never again will I buy high-heeled shoes.
Eles não têm nada.
    They have nothing.
Nunca o vi na minha vida.
    I have never seen him in my life.
Ele já não mora no Porto.
    He no longer lives in Oporto.

Hoje ainda não comi.
> I haven't eaten yet today.

Be aware of another translation of **já não**, as for example:

Já não o via há tantos anos!
> I hadn't seen him for so many years!

Note the use of double negatives in Portuguese.

30 'Já'

Já means 'already' when used in the past, but it appears much more frequently in Portuguese than 'already' does in English. For example:

Já comeu? Have you eaten?

When **já** is used in the present tense it means 'soon' or as per example:

Eu já vou. I am coming.

Here are some other uses or meanings:

já e já   straight away
desde já   from this moment on

Já não quero isso.
> I don't want that any more.

Já agora aproveito para comprar . . .
> While I am here (at it) I may as well buy . . .

Já que a sorte a trouxe aqui . . .
> Since (seeing that) Luck brought you here . . .

Exercise 21

1 Você quer tomar chá ou café?
2 Nem quero chá nem café. Prefiro um sumo de laranja.
3 Ou vou ao cinema ou fico em casa, a ver televisão, ainda não tenho a certeza.
4 Nunca vi uma exposiçao tão bem organizada.
5 Ele não tem escrúpulos nenhuns.
6 Nunca mais compro aparelhos eléctricos em segunda mão.
7 Você não tem nada a ver com isso.
8 Aqui ninguém fala inglês.
9 Eu não sei nada.
10 Não fomos a lado nenhum.

Vocabulary

café	coffee
sumo de laranja	orange juice
	(*in Brazil:* **suco de laranja**)
ficar	to stay, remain
ainda	yet, still
não tenho a certeza	I am not sure
	(*in Brazil:* **não estou certo/a**)
exposição	exhibition
escrúpulos	scruples
aparelhos eléctricos	electrical appliances
segunda mão	second-hand
não ter nada a ver com . . .	to have nothing to do with
sei	I know (*present tense of* **saber**)
fomos	we went (*past definite of* **ir**)
lado nenhum	nowhere, anywhere

30a Other indefinite adjectives and pronouns, variable and invariable

Note the feminine and plural forms in these:

certo, certa; certos, certas certain
outro, outra; outros, outras other
pouco, pouca little; **poucos, poucas** few
todo, toda; todos, todas every, all
algum, alguma; alguns, algumas some (*also* 'any' *used in questions*)
um, uma; uns, umas one, some (*often used in place of* **algum, algumas**)
tanto, tanta so much; **tantos, tantas** so many
tal, tais such
qualquer, quaisquer any (*of a choice – used in affirmative, negative or interrogative sentences*)
ambos, ambas both
alguém somebody ('anybody' *when used in questions*)
cada each
tudo everything

31 Comparison of adjectives and adverbs

The comparative

The comparative is usually formed by **mais** ('more') or **menos** ('less') plus the adjective, plus **do que** (or merely **que**):

Ela é mais bonita do que a irmã.
    She is prettier than her sister, *or*
Ela é mais bonita que a irmã.
Ela tem menos dinheiro do que eu.
    She has less money than I.

tão . . . como as . . . as
Ela é tão rica como eu. She is as rich as I.

tanto . . . como, tanta . . . como; tantos(as) . . . como as much/many . . . as
Tem tanto dinheiro como eu. She has as much money as I.

In Brazil, for 'as . . . as', say **tão . . . quanto** (or **tanto . . . quanto**, which is also occasionally used in Portugal).

The superlative

The superlative is formed by putting the articles **o, a os, as** before **mais, menos** 'more', 'less'. Thus they become 'the most', 'the least'. For example:

Ela é a mais bonita. She is the prettiest.

The superlative 'very' can be rendered by **muito**, and 'extremely' by adding **-íssimo** to the adjective after dropping the final vowel. For example:

Ela é muito bonita. She is very pretty.

lindo (beautiful)→**lindíssimo** (extremely beautiful)
barato (cheap)→**baratíssimo** (extremely cheap)

Some irregular superlatives

fácil (easy)→**facílimo**
rico (rich)→**riquíssimo**
feliz (happy)→**felicíssimo**
amável (kind)→**amabilíssimo**
pobre (poor)→**paupérrimo**

Irregular comparatives of adjectives and adverbs

bom, boa good **bem** well	**melhor** better	**o melhor** the best	**óptimo** super
mau, má, ruim bad **mal** badly, ill	**pior** worse	**o pior** the worst	**péssimo** extremely bad
grande large, big etc.	**maior** larger	**o maior** the largest	**máximo** maximum
pequeno small, little	**mais pequeno** *or* **menor**	**o mais pequeno** *or* **o menor**	**mínimo**
alto tall, high, loud	**mais alto** *or* **superior**	**o mais alto**	**supremo**
baixo low, short	**mais baixo** *or* **inferior**	**o mais baixo**	**ínfimo**
muito very – :	**mais** more/-er	**o mais** the most/-est	
pouco	**menos**	**o menos** *or* **o mínimo**	

Ele é a autoridade suprema. He is the highest authority.
O tempo está péssimo. The weather is awful.
Uma óptima ideia. A super idea.
Ela é mais linda das irmãs. She is the prettiest of the sisters.

Adverbs ending in English in *-ly* are generally formed in Portuguese by adding **-mente** to the feminine singular of the adjective. For example:

raro→**raramente** rarely
absoluto→**absolutamente** absolutely
fácil→**facilmente** easily

When two or more adverbs of this type come together **-mente** is added to the last one only. For example:

Ele falou clara e vagarosamente.
   He spoke clearly and slowly.

Exercise 22

Translate the following:

1 Does anyone speak English here?
2 Did you (*o senhor*) ask me for a spoon or a knife?
3 Neither. I asked you for a fork.
4 He has some hope.
5 Each to his own taste.
6 Everything is very expensive.
7 Have you any (any of a choice) English magazines?
8 They are both writers.
9 The dinner was awful.
10 My aunt is extremely ill.
11 He is the richest man in the world.
12 I have good news for you.
13 She is as happy as I am.
14 Camoës was the greatest Portuguese poet.

Vocabulary

pedir	to ask for
colher (*f*)	spoon
faca (*f*)	knife
nem uma nem outra	neither (one nor the other)
garfo (*m*)	fork
esperança	hope
cada qual	each (one)
gosto	taste
caro	expensive
revistas	magazines
escritores	writers
do mundo	in the world
notícias	news
para si	for you
	(*in Brazil:* **para você**)

31a 'Amar' (to love) and 'odiar' (to hate)

The verb **amar** is less commonly used in Portuguese than in English. It speaks of deep feelings, the kind that lead you to the altar. Instead, the Portuguese tend to use **gostar muito de** . . . or **adorar:**

Gosto muito de ti.
>   I like you very much, *or* I love you.
Adoro cantar.
>   I love singing.

By the same token, **odiar** is a very strong word and you'd better watch out if you ever hear it! Instead, the verb **detestar** is used:

Adoro a Inglaterra mas detesto o frio e a chuva.
>   I love England but I hate the cold and the rain.

The following piece, 'Cultural Shock', illustrates the difference between Portuguese and English:

Quando vim a Londres, pela primeira vez, ouvi o condutor do autocarro chamar-me 'amor' quando me pedia que bilhete eu queria. Fiquei visivelmente chocada e corei até às raizes do cabelo.

condutor do autocarro	bus conductor
corei	I blushed
raíz	root
cabelo (*sing.*)	hair

PRACTISE!

In association with this exercise, have a look at the section on 'Clothes and colours', page 219.

Um senhor muito chato entra numa loja . . .

Empregada	Bom dia. Faz favor?
Freguês	Bom dia, desejo comprar uma gravata que vi na montra.
Empregada	Sim senhor. Pode me descrever a gravata que viu, se faz favor.
Freguês	Bem, creio que é às riscas. Talvez não. Parece-me que a que eu vi tinha pintinhas.
Empregada	Uma grande diferença!
Freguês	Bem, a diferença está na cor.
Empregada	E de que cor era a gravata que viu?
Freguês	Julgo que era azul, mas não tenho a certeza. Em todo o caso, eu não gosto de azul; prefiro encarnado, da cor do Benfica.
Empregada	Tenho aqui uma encarnada, às pintinhas que veio da Itália.
Freguês	Não quero nada da Itália. De qualquer outro país menos da Itália.
Empregada	Então porquê?
Freguês	Então a senhora não sabe que eles nos venceram no futebol?
Empregada	O que tem a ver isso com a gravata? E a propósito de gravata. Tenho aqui uma de xadrez que veio da Inglaterra.
Freguês	Não gosto; pareço um homem que vai tocar a gaita de foles. De qualquer modo, minha senhora, eu prefiro comprar coisas portuguesas. Haja patriotismo!
Empregada	Há aqui alguma coisa que lhe agrade?
Freguês	Não, não vejo nada.
Empregada	O senhor é muito esquisito.
Freguês	Pois sou; mas não sou malcriado.
Empregada	*(entredentes)* Mas é chato. *(em voz alta)* Tenho aqui uma verde e encarnada, muita bonita. Ficava-lhe bem.

Freguês	E eu vou andar com a bandeira portuguesa ao pescoço?
Empregada	*(já irritada)* Mas afinal, o que é que o senhor deseja?
Freguês	Nada. E agora que a chuva já passou vou-me embora. Para a próxima, vou escolher uma camisa.
Empregada	As nossas camisas não são nada boas. Vá a outra loja.

chato/a	*(slang) n:* a nuisance; *adj:* boring, tiresome
montra	shop window
descrever	to describe
que viu	*past of* **ver** to see: that you saw
creio que é às riscas	I believe that it has stripes
talvez não	may be (perhaps)
creio que **parece-me que** **julgo que**	I think that . . . , it seems to me . . . that, I believe that
penso que, **acho que**	*(two more ways of saying 'I think that',* *etc., not found in this text)*
a que eu vi	the one I saw
tinha pintinhas	had polka dots
cor	colour
não tenho a certeza	I am not sure
em todo o caso	anyway
Benfica	*the well-known Portuguese football club*
veio	*past of* **vir** to come
menos	*(here:)* except
nos venceram	they defeated us
o que tem a ver isso com . . .	what has that to do with . . .
xadrez	checkered cloth (*also:* chess)
gaita de foles	bagpipes
de qualquer modo	anyway
haja patriotismo	let there be patriotism

que lhe agrade	that pleases you
vejo	*present of* **ver** to see: I see
esquisito	fussy
malcriado/a	rude
entredentes	(muttering) between (her) teeth
em voz alta	aloud
ficava-lhe bem	it should suit you
bandeira portuguesa	Portuguese flag
ao pescoço	(hanging) from (my) neck
mas, afinal	but, after all
agora que a chuva já passou	now that the rain has stopped *(lit.* passed, gone)
vou-me embora	I'm going
para a próxima	next time
escolher	to choose
não são nada boas	they aren't good at all

Exercise P. 7

Answer the questions, and check your answers by reference to the preceding dialogue:

1 Por que razão se chama 'chato' a este homem?
2 Descreva as gravatas todas que ele viu.
3 Que cor disse ele que era a sua favorita? E porquê?
4 Porque não quis ele (didn't want) a gravata italiana?
5 Qual foi a razão para ele não querer a gravata de xadrez?
6 Repita a expressão que este freguês usou como patriota.
7 Que lhe disse a empregada já desesperada?
8 E a resposta (reply) dele?
9 O que lhe chamou ela entredentes?
10 Do que lhe fez lembrar (what reminded him of) as cores encarnada e verde?
11 Finalmente, qual era a razão dele para estar naquela loja?
12 Que conselho (advice) deu-lhe a empregada?

32 The future and conditional tenses (I will, I would)

These tenses are very easily formed and conjugated. With only three exceptions, the appropriate endings are added to the infinitive of all verbs whether regular or irregular, as shown in the following tables.

Future tense

	falar (to speak) *(regular)*	**ter** (to have) *(irregular)*	**ir** (to go) *(irregular)*
eu	fala**rei**	te**rei**	i**rei**
tu	fala**rás**	te**rás**	i**rás**
você	fala**rá**	te**rá**	i**rá**
ele, ela	fala**rá**	te**rá**	i**rá**
nós	fala**remos**	te**remos**	i**remos**
vocês	fala**rão**	te**rão**	i**rão**
eles, elas	fala**rão**	te**rão**	i**rão**

Conditional tense

eu	fala**ria**	te**ria**	i**ria**
tu	fala**rias**	te**rias**	i**rias**
você	fala**ria**	te**ria**	i**ria**
ele, ela	fala**ria**	te**ria**	i**ria**
nós	fala**ríamos**	te**ríamos**	i**ríamos**
vocês	fala**riam**	te**riam**	i**riam**
eles, elas	fala**riam**	te**riam**	i**riam**

The exceptions:
dizer to say, **fazer** to make, to do, **trazer** to bring

The future and conditional endings for these three verbs are exactly the same as those shown in bold in the tables above. The only difference is that the infinitive to which the endings are added is modified as follows:

dizer *becomes*   **dir**ei, -as, -a, -emos, -ão *(future)*
                         diria, -ias, -ia, íamos, -iam *((conditional)*

fazer *becomes*   **far**ei, -as, -a, -emos, -ão *(future)*
                         faria, -ias,-ia, íamos,-iam *(conditional)*

trazer *becomes*   **trar**ei, -as, -a, -emos, -ão *(future)*
                         traria, -ias, -ia, íamos, -iam *(conditional)*

Pronominal future and conditional

When the future and conditional tenses are followed by an object pronoun, the pronoun is inserted between the stem – i. e. the infinitive – and the ending. For example:

Dar-lhe-ei I will give him . . . (*not* Darei-lhe . . .)
Eu far-lho-ia. I would do it for you.
Eles falar-me-ão. They will speak to me.

Apart from the change described above and illustrated by the preceding examples, the rules governing formation and position of pronouns apply to the future and conditional tenses in exactly the same way as explained in chapter 6.

1 The pronouns precede the verb in negative and interrogative sentences, and after certain adverbs, prepositions and conjunctions. For example:

Eles não me falarão. They will not speak to me .

2 The *r* of the infinitive is dropped before 3rd person pronouns and an accent or circumflex is placed over the remaining vowel to indicate that it retains its full sound value, as if the *r* were still present. For example:

Fá-lo-ei. I will do it.
Eles comê-lo-ão. They will eat it.

Other ways of expressing the future
(see also section 10)

1 The present tense:

In Portuguese, especially in conversation, it is much more common than in English to use the present tense to express a future intention or action. For example:

Saio amanhã,
> I'll go out tomorrow. (I'm going out tomorrow.)

2 Use of **ir** + infinitive:

Just as in English, it is possible and common in Portuguese to use the present tense of **ir** (to go) with an infinitive to express future intention. For example:

Vou sair amanhã. I'm going to go out tomorrow.

3 Use of **haver de** + infinitive:

This is another method of expressing a strong intention to perform a future action and it has, therefore, the effect of the future tense. For example:

Você há-de aprender português. You will learn Portuguese.

For the full conjugation of **haver** in the present tense, see chapter 1, sections 4 and 6.

Idiomatic uses of the future and conditional tenses

1 The future and conditional tenses can be used to express the idea of 'approximately'. In a situation pertaining to the present, the future tense is used, and in a situation pertaining to the past, the conditional is used. For example:

O nosso professor terá uns cinquenta anos.
> Our teacher is about fifty years old.
Seriam cinco horas quando ele entrou.
> He came in at about 5 o'clock.

2 It is possible to use the future and conditional tenses to convey uncertainty in situations where in English it would be natural to use the expression 'to wonder whether . . . '. For example:

Será esta a rua que buscamos*?
  I wonder whether this is the street we are looking for?
(* Brazilian usage. In Portugal say **procuramos**.)

Estaria ele culpado?
  I wonder whether he was guilty?

Note that (as in the preceding examples) the future tense is used to refer to present circumstances and the conditional to refer to past events.

Use of the imperfect to replace the conditional

The imperfect tense can be used as a substitute for the conditional when the meaning is 'I would' etc. For example:

Gostava de ir ao Brasil = Gostaria de ir ao Brasil.
  I would like to go to Brazil.

However, the imperfect cannot be used to replace the conditional when the conditional is used in one of the idiomatic senses described above. (See also section 27.)

Exercise 23

Translate the following:

1 When will you write to him?
2 He has to work hard.
3 We shall not take it.
4 I shall begin my story.
5 Who will win?
6 We shall arrive (in the) next month.
7 Was it (Would it be) true?
8 Eu diria que ele está a mentir.
9 Não me esquecerei de ti.
10 Faria tudo por ela
11 Eles dar-lhe-ão a minha nova morada.
12 Hei-de ir ao Japão.
13 Tenho de ir ao dentista.
14 Será muito caro?

Vocabulary

escrever	to write
muito	hard
começar	to begin
ganhar	to win
chegar	to arrive
verdade	true
mentir	to lie
nova	new
esquecer-se	to forget
Japão	Japan
dentista	dentist
caro	expensive

CONVERSATION

Um lugar ao sol/A place in the sun

António Ando à procura de casa no Algarve, mas não encontro nada em conta. Devia ter comprado há anos quando o Algarve ainda não era tão conhecido no estrangeiro.

Carlos Você já pôs um anúncio no jornal?

António Sim, já pus mas não recebi nenhuma resposta de interesse. É sempre a mesma história: as casas de que gosto são caras demais, e aquelas que são baratas precisam de muitas obras e são muito longe do mar. Quanto aos apartamentos, fazem-me lembrar caixas de fósforos.

Carlos Você é muito exigente. Já sabe se quer coisa boa tem de pagar, especialmente num sítio como o Algarve.

António Sim, já sei; no entanto continuarei a tentar. Ainda tenho esperanças de arranjar uma casinha de pescadores à beira-mar com um pequeno jardim com três ou quatro quartos, sala, casa de jantar, cozinha e casa de banho com chuveiro, e que custe entre as vinte e vinte e cinco mil libras.

Carlos É tudo? Quando encontrar essa raridade, veja lá se arranja duas; eu até lhe pagaria uma comissão com muito prazer.

Learn the following expressions

Ando à procura . . . I am looking for . . .
  (*In Portuguese there are a number of nouns taken from verbs -
  in this case from* **procurar** to look for)

em conta reasonably priced

Devia ter comprado há anos.
  I should have bought (it) years ago.

tão conhecido so well-known

caras demais too dear (*alternative:* **demasiado caras**)

quanto a . . . as to . . . (as for)

fazem-me lembrar . . . they remind me of . . .
  (*literally* they make me remember . . .)

muito exigente very demanding, hard to please

Já sabe. You know.

Já sei. I know. (I am well aware.)

no entanto nevertheless

Ainda tenho esperanças. I still have hopes.

casinha de pescadores a little fishermen's cottage
  (*The diminutive suffixes* **-inho/a, -zinho/a, -zito/a, -ito/a** *are
  often used in Portuguese, denoting smallness, affection or
  pity.*)

e que custe . . . and which costs . . .
  (*The use of the subjunctive is explained in chapter 9*)

É tudo? Is that all?

Veja lá se arranja duas. See if you find (get) two.
  (**lá** *meaning 'there' is often used in an abstract sense in
  colloquial speech, much as the English say 'Look here.'*)

E eu até lhe pagaria. I would even pay you.
  (**até** *meaning 'until', also means 'even' in this context.*)

Other vocabulary

encontrar	to find, to meet
no estrangeiro	abroad
estrangeiro/a	foreigner
Já pôs . . ?	Have you put . . . ?
pôr *(irregular)*	to put
anúncio	advertisement
jornal	newspaper
resposta	reply, answer
história	story, history
baratas	cheap
obra	repairs (to house), construction, literary work, opus
caixa de fósforos	a box of matches
se	if, whether
querer	to want
coisa boa	a good thing
sítio	place
tentar	to try, to attempt
beira-mar	by the sea
quartos	bedrooms
sala (de visitas)	sitting-room
casa de jantar	dining-room
cozinha	kitchen
chuveiro	shower
comissão	commission

Chapter 8

Introducing past participles, as a precursor to learning the perfect and pluperfect tenses. This chapter also includes:

- *reflexive verbs, plus the reciprocal form*
- *how to form the passive voice*
- *impersonal verbs*

33 The past participle (done, spoken, seen, etc)

The regular past participle is formed by changing the endings of the infinitive (**-ar**, **-er** and **-ir**) for **-ado**, **-ido** and **-ido** respectively. The forms are therefore as follows:

infinitive	*past participle*
dar	**dado** (given)
vender	**vendido** (sold)
mentir	**mentido** (lied)

Some past participles are irregular; these are listed below:

infinitive	*past participle*
pôr to put	**posto**
abrir to open	**aberto**
fazer to do, to make	**feito**
escrever to write	**escrito**

dizer to say, to tell	**dito**
vir to come	**vindo**
ver to see	**visto**
pagar to pay	**pago**
gastar to spend	**gasto**
ganhar to earn, to win, to gain	**ganho**

Some verbs have two past participles: a regular form which remains invariable and is used with the auxiliary verb **ter** to form compound tenses, and an irregular form which can be used as an adjective with the auxiliary verbs **ser** and **estar**. When used as an adjective, the participle agrees with the noun it qualifies in number and gender. The most important 'double past participle' forms are given below:

infinitive	*regular*	*irregular*
aceitar to accept	**aceitado**	**aceito, aceite**
acender to light	**acendido**	**aceso**
enxugar to dry	**enxugado**	**enxuto**
expulsar to expel	**expulsado**	**expulso**
juntar to join	**juntado**	**junto**
limpar to clean	**limpado**	**limpo**
matar to kill	**matado**	**morto**
morrer to die	**morrido**	**morto**
prender to arrest	**prendido**	**preso**
romper to tear	**rompido**	**roto**
suspender to suspend	**suspendido**	**suspenso**

A roupa está quáse enxuta.
    The clothes are nearly dry.
Eu já tinha enxugado a louça.
    I had already dried the dishes.
A luz está acesa.
    The light is on.
Ele já tinha acendido o fogão.
    He had already lit the fire.

34 The perfect/pluperfect tenses

These compound tenses are formed, as in English, with the auxiliary **ter** (to have) and the past participle of the main verb. The perfect uses the verb **ter** in the present indicative and expresses an action carried from the past up to the present or almost up to the present. For example:

Tenho falado. I have been speaking.

The perfect must not be confused with the past definite ('I have spoken') which expresses an action completed in the past. (You will remember that the Portuguese past definite is not a compound tense – it is simply **falei** 'I spoke'.)

The pluperfect has the verb **ter** in the imperfect and indicates an action in the past prior to another past action, the same as in English:

Tinha falado. I had spoken.

Here are a few examples showing all four past tenses.

Ontem falei com a tua irmã.
   Yesterday I spoke to your sister. *(past definite)*
Falava com a tua mãe.
   I was speaking to your mother. *(imperfect)*
Ultimamente tenho falado muito francês.
   I have been speaking a lot of French lately. *(perfect)*
Já tinha falado com o meu patrão antes de você me pedir para o fazer.
   I had already spoken to my boss before you asked me to do it. *(pluperfect)*

There is a fifth tense, also called the pluperfect, which is not a compound tense and is therefore in Portuguese **mais que perfeito simples** while the pluperfect shown above is called **mais que perfeito composto**. The simple pluperfect is seldom used in colloquial speech. (See the Appendix.)

PRACTISE!

Uma senhora, que tinha visto um ladrão fugir duma loja, foi à esquadra dar pormenores.

Polícia   O nome da senhora, faz favor; morada, lugar onde nasceu e data do seu nascimento.

Senhora Antunes   Chamo-me Maria Antunes, moro na Rua das Flores, no. 18, 1º Esq. e nasci em Viana do Castelo a 18 de outubro de 1930.

Polícia   . . . nome de pai e mãe.

Senhora Antunes   O Senhor Guarda, mas isso é necessário?

Polícia   É, senão não tinha perguntado.

Senhora Antunes   Bem, a minha mãe era Antónia Maria Antunes, a 'padeira'.

Polícia   Não estamos interessados em alcunhas. E o seu pai?

Senhora Antunes   Sei lá! Foi antes do meu tempo!

Polícia   Ora bem! Pode descrever-me o ladrão que viu?

Senhora Antunes   Vi-o muito bem. Era alto. Não. Estou enganada. Era mais baixo que alto. Moreno. Pensando bem, eu não podia ver-lhe a cara porque ele tinha um lenço por sobre o rosto.

Polícia   (*em voz baixa*) (Estes pormenores vão ajudar-me muito, não há dúvida nenhuma.) Gordo ou magro?

Senhora Antunes   Gordo. Mais gordo do que eu.

Polícia   Cor do cabelo?

Senhora Antunes   Sei lá! Talvez loiro . . . Estava muito escuro.

Polícia   Estava escuro? Como é possível quando o roubo aconteceu pela manhã?

Senhora Antunes   Ah, Senhor Guarda, então foi outro roubo que eu vi.

Polícia   Na mesma loja? Um de manhã e outro de tarde?

Senhora Antunes   Pois é verdade. Agora há tantos roubos!

Polícia   Desculpe-me minha senhora, mas eu tenho que entrevistar outras pessoas. Obrigada por ter vindo. Adeus!

ladrão	thief
fugir	run away, flee
esquadra	police station
pormenores *(m pl)*	details
nasceu	*v.* **nascer** to be born
nascimento	birth
1º Esq.	1st floor on the left (left-hand flat)
Senhor Guarda	*(the correct way to address a policeman)* Officer.
senão	otherwise
padeira	the baker (*f*), the baker's wife
alcunha	nickname
Sei la!	How should I know? God knows!
Ora bem!	Well now!
moreno	dark (olive skin) complexion
pensando bem	on second thoughts
cara, rosto	face
lenço	handkerchief
não há dúvida nenhuma	there is no doubt at all
cabelo	hair
roubo	theft
aconteceu	*v.* **acontecer** to happen
Pois é verdade	So, it is; that is so; indeed!
entrevistar	to interview

Exercise P. 8

Answer the following questions, checking against the dialogue:

1 Porque foi a senhora à Polícia?
2 Como se chamava ela? Onde tinha ela nascido e quando?
3 Qual era a morada dela?
4 Que alcunha tinha a mãe dela?
5 Qual foi a resposta dela quando o polícia lhe perguntou o nome do pai?
6 A senhora Antunes deu pormenores correctos a respeito do ladrão? (Dê exemplos.)
7 Porque não pôde ela ver o rosto do ladrão?
8 Quando tinha acontecido o roubo?
9 Na sua opinião, acha que a Sra. Antunes tinha visto algum roubo?
10 Que conclusão tirou deste caso?

35 Reflexive verbs

A reflexive verb is one in which the object of the verb is the same person or thing as the subject, where the action reflects back on the subject. Reflexive verbs are much more common in Portuguese than in English. They are formed by combining the reflexive pronouns **me, te, se** etc, with the appropriate part of the verb. The pronoun comes before or after the verb according to the rules explained in section 25. Although the reflexive pronoun can be translated as 'myself', 'yourself', etc, it is not usually natural in English to translate it at all.

Some reflexive verbs:

levantar-se to get up
lembrar-se de to remember
esquecer-se de to forget
sentar-se to sit down
lavar-se to wash oneself, to have a wash
barbear-se to shave oneself
deitar-se to go to bed, to lie down
vestir-se to get dressed
despir-se to get undressed
pentear-se to comb one's hair
banhar-se to bathe
divertir-se to enjoy oneself
habituar-se a to get used to
sentir-se to feel
decidir-se a to decide to

Não me lembrava da tua morada.
    I could not remember your address.
Eles vão-se lavar. They are going to get washed.
Divertimo-nos muito na sua festa.
    We enjoyed ourselves very much at your party.
Por favor sente-se. Please sit down.
Avie-se. *or* **Despache-se.** Hurry up.
Você enganou-se. You made a mistake.
Sirva-se. Help yourself.

*Use of **mesmo and próprio** to translate 'myself, 'yourself', etc*

In English, the forms 'myself', 'yourself' etc are also used to give emphasis to the subject. This is expressed in Portuguese *not* by the reflexive pronoun but by the use of the adjectives **mesmo** and **próprio**, which agree with the subject in number and gender:

Eu própria lhe contei a história.
    I myself told him the story.
Nós mesmos não queríamos ir.
    We ourselves did not want to go.
Ele mesmo veio falar comigo.
    He came himself to speak to me.

36 The reciprocal form

Reciprocal actions, although different from reflexive verbs, require the use of the reflexive pronoun. For example:

Nós encontrámo-nos por acaso. We met by chance.
Eles amam-se. They love each other.
Elas não se conhecem. They don't know each other.
Nunca nos vimos. We have never seen each other.

To avoid ambiguity between the reflexive and reciprocal forms, the phrase **um ao outro** (one another) is sometimes added to make it clear that the verb is reciprocal. This is especially important in cases where the verb is naturally reflexive. The phrase **um ao outro** varies according to the number and gender of the subjects involved:

um ao outro (two *m sing.* subjects)
uma à outra (two *f sing.* subjects)
uns aos outros (more than two *m pl* or mixed *m & f pl*
subjects)
umas às outras (more than two *f pl* subjects)
and so on.

Consider the following: **Eles enganam-se** would normally mean 'They are making a mistake'. But it could mean 'They are deceiving each other'. To make the latter meaning absolutely clear it is necessary to add the appropriate form of **um ao outro**. For example:

A minha irmã e o cunhado enganam-se um ao outro.
My sister and brother-in-law deceive each other.

37 The passive voice and 'se' as impersonal subject pronoun

The passive voice is formed with the verb **ser** and the past participle, which must agree in number and gender with the subject. It is not as much used as the English passive voice, which is often translated by the Portuguese active voice plus the indeterminate pronoun **se**, that is, reflexively – **se** forms an impersonal subject pronoun. For example:

Aqui fala-se português.
Portuguese is spoken here.
Disseram-me que . . .
I was told that . . . (*literally* They told me that . . .)
Diz-se que ela é muito rica.
It is said that she is very rich, *or*
Dizem que ela é muito rica.
It is said that she is very rich. (*literally* They say that she is very rich.)

Vê-se muita gente nas ruas no Natal.
Many people are seen in the streets at Christmas.
Aqui vendem-se jornais.
Newspapers are sold here.

The passive voice is followed by the preposition **por** ('by'), combined with the articles in the usual way:

A carta foi escrita pela irmã.
The letter was written by (his/her) sister.
Ela é amada por todos.
She is loved by everybody.

Exercise 24

Translate the following:

1 Ela já tinha estudado português quando era criança.
2 Este ano tem havido muitos desastres de avião.
3 A mulher já estava morta quando o médico chegou.
4 As mesas já estavam postas mas os convidados ainda não tinham chegado.
5 Eu nunca tinha visto tanta gente na minha vida.
6 Ela foi expulsa da escola.
7 Diz-se que a firma Agiota & Co. vai falir.
8 Não se deve enganar os outros.
9 Elas ainda não se tinham lavado.
10 Tem feito muito mau tempo.

Vocabulary

criança	child
desastres	accidents, disasters
convidados	guests
tanta gente	so many people
vida	life
falir	to fold up, to go bankrupt
enganar	to cheat
fazer bom/mau tempo	to have good/bad weather

38 Impersonal verbs

There are a number of verbs which are used in the 3rd person singular only. The most common of these are **há** (there is, there are) and expressions describing the weather (such as **chove** it is raining, **neva** it is snowing). Other examples are:

Faz calor (It is hot), **Faz frio** (It is cold), **Faz sol** (It is sunny), **Faz vento** (It is windy).

Exercise 25

Translate the following:

1 Eles sentiam-se desanimados.
2 Levantei-me muito cedo.
3 Ele nunca se lembra dos meus anos.
4 Ela vestiu-se à pressa.
5 Ele cheira mal porque nunca se lava.
6 Como se diz 'table' em português?
7 Eles olharam-se um ao outro.
8 Sirva-se enquanto a comida está quente.
9 Não nos conhecemos.
10 Eu queixei-me à polícia.
11 Vá-se embora.
12 Faz sol.
13 Esqueci-me dele.
14 Aqui vendem-se jornais ingleses.

Vocabulary

desanimados	disappointed
cedo	early
meus anos	my birthday
pressa	hurry
cheirar	to smell
olhar	to look at
comida	food
queixar-se	to complain
ir-se embora	to go away, to leave

Exercise 26

Translate the following:

1 I remember him.
2 I was not feeling well.
3 We complained about the food.
4 It has been raining a lot this year.
5 I had already mailed the letter.
6 A lot of wine is drunk in Portugal but the Portuguese never get drunk.
7 The window was open.
8 The lottery was won by a poor woman.
9 My skirt was torn.
10 They were all arrested.
11 They looked at each other.
12 I have not travelled (been travelling) this year.
13 One hears a lot of British music in Portugal.
14 I do not want to help myself.
15 We saw each other by chance.
16 Newspapers are sold here.

Vocabulary

pôr a carta no correio	to mail a letter
embriagar-se	to get drunk
lotaria	lottery
saia	skirt
viajar	to travel
rasgar	to tear
ganhar	to win
prender, presos	to arrest, arrested (*pl*)

CONVERSATION

No restaurante/At the restaurant

o senhor Carvalho	Boa noite, tem uma mesa livre?
o criado de mesa	O senhor não reservou?
o senhor Carvalho	Não, não tive tempo, foi uma coisa resolvida à última hora.
o criado	Vou ver. Quantas pessoas são?
o senhor Carvalho	Quatro. Preferia uma mesa ao pé da janela, pois está muito calor.
o criado	Lamento muito mas as mesas ao pé das janelas estão todas reservadas. Esta aqui agrada-lhe?
o senhor Carvalho	Que remédio! Traga-nos a ementa por favor e a lista dos vinhos. O que nos recomenda?
o criado	Recomendo-lhes o prato do dia que é especialidade cá da casa 'bacalhau de cebolada', ou então 'porco com ameijoas à alentejana' que é um grande petisco português.
o senhor Carvalho	Pois bem, traga esse para mim, 'bacalhau de cebolada' para a minha filha um bife 'à transmontana' para a minha mulher, e para o meu amigo 'frango na púcara'.
o criado	Que legumes?
o senhor Carvalho	Ervilhas e batatas fritas para dois, puré de batata e feijão verde para outro e arroz e salada de alface e pepino para mim.
o criado	E para beber, o que desejam?

o senhor Carvalho	Vinho da casa. Uma garrafa de tinto e uma de branco. Traga também dois cafèzinhos - um simples e um com leite para terminar o jantar pois não queremos sobremesa. Queria também que me trouxesse a conta porque estamos com muita pressa; vamos a um concerto e não podemos chegar atrasados.

No hotel/At the hotel

o senhor Jones	Boa tarde. Chamo-me Jones. Escrevi a marcar um quarto de casal e um quarto para pessoa só.
a recepcionista	Um momento se faz favor. Ora aqui está . . . Senhor Jones, dois quartos para o dia dezoito. Há aqui um problema; aparentemente o meu colega deu estes quartos a outras pessoas porque pensava que os senhores não viessem. Nós só reservamos os quartos até ao meio-dia. Como devem compreender esta é a época dos turistas e há falta de acomodação.
o senhor Jones	Que falta de consideração! Não sabe que hoje em dia os aviões chegam e partem quando lhes apetecem? Não é nossa culpa se chegamos atrasados. Nós já lhe tínhamos escrito a fazer esta marcação e os senhores responderam a confirmá-la. Isto não se pode admitir. Estamos cansados e aborrecidos e agora não temos quartos. Eu daqui não saio até que me arranjem acomodação.

a recepcionista Peço imensa desculpa por este lapso da nossa parte. Vou ver o que se pode arranjar. *(A recepcionista depois de uns minutos, regressa.)*
Estamos com sorte. Falei com o gerente que me disse para lhes dar o apartamento de luxo que está normalmente reservado para certas entidades e ocasiões especiais. Os senhores podem tê-lo pelo mesmo preço que os quartos que tinham reservado, lhes custariam. É claro que só o podemos dar por duas noites. Depois se verá.

o senhor Jones Não faz mal. Estamos gratos por este gesto amável. A que horas servem o pequeno-almoço?

a recepcionista Das sete às nove e meia. Desejam meia--pensão ou pensão completa?

o senhor Jones Preferimos pensão completa. E gostaríamos que nos acordassem às oito em ponto com três chávenas de chá à inglesa.

a recepcionista Muito bem; aqui está a vossa chave. O empregado vai levar-vos as malas.

Vocabulary

AT THE RESTAURANT

Foi uma coisa resolvida à última hora.
  It was a last-minute thing.
ao pé da
  near, close to
Esta aqui agrada-lhe?
  Will this one do?
bacalhau de cebolada
  cod in onions (**bacalhau,** salted cod, is the national dish)
à transmontana
  cooked in the fashion of Trás-os-Montes, a northern
  province of Portugal
porco com ameijoas à alentejana
  pork with clams in the fashion of Alentejo, a province
  south of the River Tagus
frango na púcara
  traditional Portuguese dish, 'chicken in the pot', which
  is cooked in an earthenware pot with herbs.

legumes	vegetables
ervilhas	peas
batatas fritas	fried potatoes
puré de batata	mashed potato
feijão verde	green beans
arroz	rice
alface	lettuce
pepino	cucumber
garrafa	bottle, *also* carafe
tinto	red
branco	white
cafèzinhos	coffees *(diminutive form *)*
um café simples	a black coffee *(also known as* **uma bica)**
café com leite	white coffee *(slang:* **garoto)**
pois	as, for, because
sobremesa	dessert
a conta	the bill

AT THE HOTEL

marcar	to book
um quarto de casal	a double bedroom
para pessoa só	single room
falta de	shortage of
Que falta de consideração!	What lack of consideration!
quando lhes apetece	when they feel like it
hoje em dia	nowadays
Não é nossa culpa.	It is not our fault.
marcação	booking
Isto não se pode admitir.	This is unacceptable.
Eu daqui não saio . . .	I am not leaving here . . .
até que me arranjem . . .	until you find me . . .
peço imensa desculpa	I am so very sorry
lapso da nossa parte	oversight on our part
o que se pode arranjar	what can be done
gerente	manager
certas entidades	certain personalities (VIPs)
depois se verá	we shall see after that
Não faz mal.	It does not matter.
gesto amável	kind gesture
pequeno-almoço	breakfast (*in Brazil*: **café da manhã**)
meia pensão	half board
pensão completa	full board
acordar	to wake someone up
chávenas de chá	cups of tea (*in Brazil:* **xícara.** This word is still in use in regional Portuguese and in culinary language.)
chave	key
levar-vos as malas	to take the suitcases for you

*The affectionate temperament of the Portuguese is reflected in their language by the diminutives **-inho, -zinho, -ito, -zito.** These are added to the noun or object to express affection, commiseration or smallness. Thus you may find **favor** changed to **favorzinho,** and **obrigada** changed to **obrigadinha.**

Chapter 9

In this chapter we reach the subjunctive: present, imperfect, future, perfect and pluperfect.

- uses of the subjunctive
- regular, irregular and exceptional forms in the various tenses
- 'if' clauses explained

39 The present subjunctive

The present subjunctive is not a difficult tense to form and conjugate. If you forget the final **-r** of the infinitive, you'll see that verbs belonging to the 'a' conjugation end in **e**, whereas those of the second and third conjugations ('e' and 'i') end in **a**. The following table shows the basic principle for changing from the present indicative to the subjunctive.

Regular verbs

	falar (to speak)	**comer** (to eat)	**partir** (to leave)
eu	fal**e**	com**a**	part**a**
tu	fal**es**	com**as**	part**as**
você	fal**e**	com**a**	part**a**
ele, ela	fal**e**	com**a**	part**a**
nós	fal**emos**	com**amos**	part**amos**
vocês	fal**em**	com**am**	part**am**
eles, elas	fal**em**	com**am**	part**am**

Exceptions and irregular verbs

The present subjunctive of irregular verbs is formed from the 1st person singular of the present indicative by removing the letter **o** and adding the endings **-a, -as, -a, amos, -am**. For example:

faz**er**→faç**o**→faç**a**, faç**as**, faç**a**, faç**amos**, faç**am**

There are seven exceptions to the general rule as follows:

ser	estar	dar	haver	saber	querer	ir
seja	esteja	dê	haja	saiba	queira	vá
sejas	estejas	dês	hajas	saibas	queiras	vás
seja	esteja	dê	haja	saiba	queira	vá
sejamos	estejamos	dêmos	hajamos	saibamos	queiramos	vamos
sejam	estejam	dêem	hajam	saibam	queiram	vão

See also the table of verbs in the Appendix.

40 Uses of the subjunctive mood

Generally speaking the subjunctive expresses a possibility, something yet to happen, or something contrary to actual fact. It corresponds to 'may', 'should' and 'might' in English.

The subjunctive is used in subordinate clauses:

1 After the verb in the main clause expresses doubt, command, denial, wish, prohibition, permission, hope, request, regret, and verbs of emotion (to be sorry, to be sad, to be happy, to fear):

Main clause	*Subordinate clause*
Quero	**que você saia.**
I want	you to go out. (*literally* that you should go out)

Duvido que ele venha hoje.

> I doubt whether he will come today. (*literally* that he may come)

Espero que ela esteja melhor.

> I hope she is better.

Lamento que não possamos vir.

> I regret that we are not able to come.

Folgo muito que seja assim.

> I am so happy that it is so.

Temo que haja uma guerra.

> I fear there may be a war.

Temos pena que eles não falem português.

> We are sorry that they don't speak Portuguese.

2 In impersonal sentences:

É preciso que vocês estudem muito. It is necessary for you to study hard. (You must study hard.)

'E preciso' corresponds to the French 'il faut'.

É provável que eu vá ao Japão.

> It is probable that I will go to Japan.

3 After verbs in the negative which express an opinion or thought:

Não acho que ele seja malcriado.

> I don't think he is ill-mannered.

Não creio que o governo vá mudar.

> I don't believe the government is going to change.

Note that the affirmative is rendered in the indicative:

Creio que o governo vai mudar.

> I believe the government is going to change.

4 After indefinite antecedents (i.e. when the subject is general or not defined):

Há aqui alguém que fale inglês?

> Is there anyone here who speaks English?

Procuro uma casa que seja barata.

> I am looking for a house that is cheap.

Compare the last with:

Procuro a casa que está anunciada no jornal.

> I am looking for the house that is advertised in the
> paper.

Here the subject is specifically identified and the indicative
should be used.

5 After **talvez, tomara** and **oxalá** (see chapter 5, conversation
vocabulary):

Talvez seja verdade.

> Maybe it is true.

Oxalá amanhã não chova.

> I hope it does not rain tomorrow.

Tomara que ele não venha.

> I hope/ wish he doesn't come.

Note that **tomara** is used in northern Portugal and Brazil,
while **oxalá** (due to its Arabic derivation) is more frequently
heard in Lisbon and the south.

6 After the following conjunctions (adverbial clauses):

a não ser que unless
antes que before
até que until
ainda que although, though
embora though, although
mesmo que even if
se bem que even though, although
contanto que provided that
para que so that, in order that
sem que without

Janto consigo contanto que você pague a conta.

> I shall dine with you provided you pay the bill.

Vamos agora sair antes que chova.

> We are going to leave now before it rains.

Exercise 27

Translate the following:

1 É preciso que eles estudem muito.
2 Oxalá eles não venham tarde.
3 Talvez eu saia amanhã.
4 Quero que você faça isso imediatamente.
5 Diga-lhe que não entre até que eu o chame.
6 Espero que a sua mulher esteja melhor.
7 Não acho que ele seja um bom jogador de futebol.
8 Queremos um homem que tenha a coragem das suas convicções.
9 Quer queira quer não queira, tenho de assistir à reunião amanhã.
10 Tell him not to go to the meeting.
11 Although I don't speak Portuguese very well, I understand everything.
12 Do you want me to bring you the wine list?
13 It is better for me to go now.
14 I don't think there are any newspapers today.
15 They are sorry you cannot come tonight.
16 Please don't make any noise.

Note: please remember that the polite form of command (imperative) is in fact a subjunctive.

Vocabulary

até	until
jogador	player
quer queira quer não queira	whether I like it or not
reunião	meeting
lista dos vinhos	wine list
barulho	noise, commotion

41 The imperfect subjunctive

The imperfect subjunctive of regular verbs is formed by removing the final letter **r** from the infinitive and adding the endings shown in the table below.

	falar (to speak)	**comer** (to eat)	**partir**(to leave)
eu	fala**sse**	come**sse**	parti**sse**
tu	fala**sses**	come**sses**	parti**sses**
você	fala**sse**	come**sse**	parti**sse**
ele, ela	fala**sse**	come**sse**	parti**sse**
nós	falá**ssemos**	comê**ssemos**	partí**ssemos**
vocês	fala**ssem**	come**ssem**	parti**ssem**
eles, elas	fala**ssem**	come**ssem**	parti**ssem**

The imperfect subjunctive of irregular verbs is formed by removing the ending **-mos** from the 1st person plural of the past definite tense (see section 23), and adding the endings shown in bold in the table above. For example:

fazer→fize|mos *(past definite)*→fize**sse**, fize**sses**, fize**ssemos**, fize**ssem**

There are no exceptions to this rule. The imperfect subjunctive of some common irregular verbs is given below.

dar→de|**mos**→de**sse**, de**sses**, dé**ssemos**, de**ssem**
haver→houve|**mos**→houve**sse**, houve**sses**, houvé**ssemos**, houve**ssem**

ser
ir }→fo|**mos**→fo**sse**, fo**sses**, fô**ssemos**, fo**ssem**

ter→tive|**mos**→tive**sse**, tive**sses**, tivé**ssemos**, tive**ssem**
vir→vie|**mos**→vie**sse**, vie**sses**, vié**ssemos**, vie**ssem**
ver→vi|**mos**→vi**sse**, vi**sses**, ví**ssemos**, vi**ssem**
estar→estive|**mos**→estive**sse**, estive**sses**, estivé**ssemos**, estive**ssem**
dizer→disse|**mos**→disse**sse**, disse**sses**, dissé**ssemos**, disse**ssem**

Use of the imperfect subjunctive

The imperfect subjunctive is used in the same circumstances as the present subjunctive when the verb in the main clause is in the past tense or conditional tense. For example:

Queria que ele arranjasse um emprego melhor.
 I wanted him to get a better job.
Disse-lhe que não se fosse embora.
 I told him not to go away.
Ele pediu-me que lhe dissesse que não podia vir.
 He asked me to tell you that he could not come.

42 The future subjunctive

The future subjunctive of the regular verbs is formed as follows:

	falar (to speak)	**comer** (to eat)	**partir** (to leave)
eu	fala**r**	come**r**	parti**r**
tu	fala**res**	come**res**	parti**res**
você	fala**r**	come**r**	parti**r**
ele, ela	fala**r**	come**r**	parti**r**
nós	fala**rmos**	come**rmos**	parti**rmos**
vocês	fala**rem**	come**rem**	parti**rem**
eles, elas	fala**rem**	come**rem**	parti**rem**

The future subjunctive of irregular verbs is formed by re-moving the ending **-mos** from the 1st person plural of the past definite tense and adding the endings shown in bold in the table above. For example:

fazer→fize|**mos**→fize**r**, fize**res**, fize**rmos**, fize**rem**

Use of the future subjunctive

The future subjunctive is used when referring to actions or events, the performance or fulfilment of which is either un-certain or dependent on the completion of another action or event which has not taken place at the time of speaking. It is introduced most commonly by the following words:

quando when, whenever
se if
enquanto que while
assim que as soon as
logo que as soon as
como as
conforme according to
o que whatever
quem whoever
aquele, aquela que whoever
aqueles, aquelas que those who

The following example makes the use of this tense easier to appreciate.

Quando nós formos a Portugal, escrever-te-emos.
    When we go to Portugal we will write to you.
(Both actions will take place in the future and one is dependent on the successful completion of the other.)

Set expressions using present and future subjunctive

There are a number of set formulae in Portuguese which follow the pattern of *present + future subjunctive*. The most common of these are listed below.

Aconteça o que acontecer . . . Whatever happens . . .
Haja o que houver . . . Whatever there may be . . .
Seja quem for . . . Whoever it may be . . . / Whoever you may be . . . (*formal*)
Diga o que quiser . . . Say what you like . . .
Seja onde for . . . Wherever it may be . . .
Faça como quiser . . . Do as you please . . .

Many other permutations are possible, using this model structure.

PRACTISE!

Ana   As férias estão quase a acabar. Quem me dera que elas nunca acabassem.

Pedro   Eu também seria mais feliz se não tivesse que trabalhar. Mas, no ano que vem vou ter este desejo, isto é, se eu obtiver a minha licenciatura.

Ana   Que sorte! E o que vais fazer?

Pedro   Vou visitar Macau, antes que ele tenha outra bandeira, assim como Hong Kong e, já que estou naquela parte do mundo, irei visitar o Japão e a China, se Deus quiser.

Ana   E quem vai pagar isso tudo?

Pedro   O meu pai, claro. Ele tinha me dito que se eu não 'chumbasse' nos exames, ele me oferecia esta viagem. Oxalá ele não falte ao prometido.

Ana   Claro que ele não vai fazer isso. Quem me dera que o meu fizesse o mesmo. Não seria bom se nós fôssemos juntos?

Pedro   Seria. Mas, mesmo que não vás comigo eu lembrar-me-ei sempre de ti. E, aconteça o que acontecer, a nossa amizade não morrerá.

Ana   Espero que não.

Quem me dera	(*simple pluperfect of* **dar**) How I wish!
obtiver	(*fut. subj. of* **obter**) if I get, obtain
licenciatura	B. A., graduation
bandeira	flag
se Deus quiser	(*fut. subj. of* **querer**) God willing
se eu não chumbasse	(*imp. subj.*) if I didn't flunk (the exams)
faltar ao prometido	to go back on his word, to fail in his promise
se fôssemos juntos	(*imp. subj. of* **ir**) if we went together
amizade (*f*)	friendship

43 Perfect and pluperfect subjunctive

These compound tenses are formed quite easily by combining the present and imperfect subjunctive of the auxiliary **ter** with the past participle as shown in the table below.

	perfect subjunctive	*pluperfect subjunctive*
eu	ten**ha** falado	tive**sse** falado
tu	ten**has** falado	tive**sses** falado
você	ten**ha** falado	tive**sse** falado
ele, ela	ten**ha** falado	tive**sse** falado
nós	tenh**amos** falado	tiv**éssemos** falado
vocês	tenh**am** falado	tive**ssem** falado
eles, elas	tenh**am** falado	tive**ssem** falado

These compound subjunctive tenses are used in the situations described under *Uses of the subjunctive mood* in section 40. The following examples illustrate this:

After verbs of emotion
Espero que tenha vindo.
    I hope he has come.

Esperava que tivesse vindo.

I hoped he had come.

After impersonal expressions

É provável que ele tenha ido a Lisboa.

It is likely that he has gone to Lisbon.

Era provável que ele tivesse ido a Lisboa.

It was likely that he had gone to Lisbon.

After verbs expressing opinion in the negative

Não creio que tenham chegado.

I don't think they have arrived.

Não pensei que tivessem chegado.

I didn't think they had arrived.

After indefinite antecedents

Há aqui alguém que tenha visto o meu irmão?

Is there anyone here who has seen my brother?

Havia lá alguém que tivesse visto o seu irmão?

Was there anyone there who had seen your brother?

After talvez, tomara and oxalá

Talvez tenham chegado.

Perhaps they have arrived.

Talvez não o tivessem ouvido.

Maybe they had not heard him.

Oxalá não tenha falado com os meus pais!

I do hope he hasn't spoken to my parents!

Oxalá me tivesses dado ouvidos!

If only you had listened to me!

Tomara que ele não tivesse vindo.

I wish he had not come.

In adverbial clauses

Dar-lhe-ei as mercadorias contanto que tenha pago a conta.

I will give you the goods provided that you have paid the bill.

Ter-lhe-ia dado as mercadorias contanto que você tivesse pago a conta.

I would have given you the goods provided you had paid the bill.

The pluperfect subjunctive is also used in 'if' clauses referring to hypothetical or impossible situations. This is explained in more detail in the next section.

44 'If' clauses

The word for 'if' in Portuguese is **se**. The sequence of tenses used with **se** is determined according to the following system:

1 Se referring to real facts

These sentences follow the pattern 'If A is true then B is true'. In such cases, **se** is followed by the indicative mood. For example:

Se ela compra uma propriedade, é porque tem dinheiro.
If she buys a property it is because she has the money.
Se o marido chegava atrasado, ela inquietava-se.
If her husband arrived late, she used to worry.

In this type of sentence it should normally be possible to substitute 'when' for 'if' without substantially changing the meaning. This is a useful identification test in 'if' sentences.

2 Se meaning 'whether'

When **se** means 'whether', it is always followed by the indicative mood. For example:

Não sei se ele vem.
I do not know whether he is coming.
Ao rei não lhe importava se morriam os súbditos.
The king did not care whether his subjects were dying.
Não me disse se eles tinham chegado.
He didn't tell me whether they had arrived.

3 Se referring to possible events which have not yet happened

In sentences involving actions or events which are possible but have not been completed or fulfilled at the time of speaking, the future subjunctive is used. For example:

Se te lembrares, traz-me pêssegos de Portugal.
   If you remember, bring me some peaches from
   Portugal.
Se formos a Portugal, trar-te-emos pêssegos.
   If we go to Portugal, we will bring you peaches.

4 **Se** referring to impossible or hypothetical events

When **se** refers to actions or events which are imaginary or speculative, such as those invented for the sake of argument, the imperfect subjunctive is used. For example:

Se fosse rico, iria dar uma volta ao mundo.
   If I were rich, I would travel round the world.
Se ela tivesse dinheiro, comprava uma propriedade.
   If she had money, she would buy a property.

When referring to actions or events in the past which might have happened but did not in fact take place, the pluperfect subjunctive is used. For example:

Se tivéssemos sabido disso, não teríamos dito nada.
   If we had known that, we would not have said
   anything.

Exercise 28

Translate the following:

1 Foi pena que ele não pudesse vir.
2 Eu queria que vocês aprendessem português tão depressa quanto possível.
3 Não vi nenhuma casa que me agradasse.
4 Talvez ele tivesse já partido.
5 Se não fosse tão caro comprávamos uma quinta no Algarve.
6 Não queríamos que vocês trouxessem presentes.
7 Não sei se chove.
8 Se chover levo um guarda-chuva.
9 Enquanto os operários não recomeçarem o trabalho não podemos aumentar a produção.
10 Vem a nossa casa quando quiseres.
11 Assim que você arranjar um emprego em Moçambique, diga-me.
12 Faça o que puder.
13 Convidem quem desejarem.
14 Aquele que quiser vir comigo que venha.

Vocabulary

tão depressa quanto possível	as soon as possible
agradar	to please
guarda-chuva	umbrella
enquanto . . . não	until
operários	workmen, factory workers
recomeçarem	to start again
aumentar	to increase
vem	come
	(familiar singular imperative)
faça	do
convidar	to invite
desejar	to wish
que venha	let him come

Exercise 29

Translate the following:

1 As soon as you *(familiar)* can, please ring me up.
2 If he were not so lazy, he would not have lost that job.
3 It was necessary for them to call the police.
4 I told them to go away.
5 Whatever you say, I don't believe she is dishonest.
6 When I retire I shall write many books.
7 You may do as you wish.
8 Whatever happens and in spite of the weather I shall always love England.
9 There was no-one who spoke English.
10 While you *(pl)* are in my house you are my guests.
11 I was sorry they were not able to come.
12 If you have lost this opportunity, it is because you wanted to.
13 Although they protested many times, the situation remained the same.

Vocabulary

preguiçoso, mandrião, mandriona *(f)*	lazy
ir-se embora	to go away
desonesta	dishonest
reformar-se, aposentar-se	retire
apesar de	in spite of
convidados	guests
oportunidade	opportunity
protestar	to complain, to protest
muitas vezes	many times
continuou na mesma	remained the same

CONVERSATION

Uma avaria de automóvel/A car breakdown

Joaquina Olá, como estás? Então por cá?

Mafalda Sim cheguei ontem, às quatro da tarde. Ainda tentei telefonar-te mas o teu telefone estava impedido.

Joaquina Pois estava. Era o meu marido que estava a fazer um telefonema para a França. Foi, por sinal, uma chamada caríssima, porque ele esteve a falar com o sócio francês dele, quáse uma hora. E tu que me contas? Vieste de barco?

Mafalda Não, por acaso não. Vim de automóvel pela França e Espanha.

Joaquina O quê? Vieste sozinha por aí fora?

Mafalda Não, não; vim com duas amigas. A viagem correu muito bem até chegarmos à vizinhança de Salamanca. De repente o carro deu um solavanco, derrapou para o sentido contrário e parou, felizmente sem nenhum embate. A surpresa foi tão grande e tudo se passou tão rapidamente que nem nos apercebemos do perigo. O susto veio depois do sucedido, por assim dizer. Descobrimos que era um furo no pneu. Infelizmente tinha me esquecido de trazer as ferramentas.

Joaquina Mas que disparate que fizeste!

Mafalda Bem sei, e jurei nunca mais fazê-lo. Enfim, lá veio um carro que parou. Calcula tu que o motorista era um médico! Fiquei consternada pois talvez ele estivesse a caminho da casa dum doente. Ele foi muito amável e mudou-nos a roda. Ainda bem que não me tinha esquecido do pneu sobresselente!

Joaquina   Também digo! Foi este o único azar que tiveram?

Mafalda   Não. Assim que passámos a fronteira – onde por sinal os funcionários da alfândega foram muito amáveis – o carro teve outra avaria.

Joaquina   Não me digas! Mas que pouca sorte!

Mafalda   É verdade! Graças a Deus encontrámos um bom mecânico que atendeu à embraiagem, afinou os travões e carregou a bateria. Foi uma despesa com que não contávamos e a falta deste dinheiro faz-nos uma grande diferença.

Joaquina   Mas naturalmente! Faria a qualquer pessoa. Olha! Vê lá que já são cinco horas. Ai, meu Deus, como o tempo voa! Tenho que me encontrar com o meu marido às cinco e meia para depois irmos à 'soirée' duma peça que tem tido muito êxito. Telefona-me amanhã para marcarmos o dia que vens a minha casa para jantar. Um dia que estejas disponível. Adeus, até amanhã.

Vocabulary

avaria	breakdown (*applies to anything out of order, like the TV, etc*)
Então por cá?	What? You over here?
tentar	to try, to attempt
impedido	engaged (*telephone*)
por sinal	as it happens, as a matter of fact
sócio	partner
contar	to tell
por acaso	actually, as a matter of fact
sozinha	alone
por aí fora	all that way
correu muito bem	went very well
vizinhança	neighbourhood, proximity of, outskirts of
de repente	suddenly
solavanco	jolt
derrapar	to skid
contrário	opposite
embate	collision (*in Brazil:* **descontrole**)
embater	to collide with
perigo	danger
susto	fright, shock
sucedido	event
por assim dizer	so to speak
furo no pneu	puncture in the tyre
infelizmente	unfortunately
ferramentas	tools
disparate	foolish mistake, silly thing, nonsense
bem sei	I know
jurei	I swore
fiquei consternada	I was dismayed, aghast (I was so embarrassed)
roda	wheel

ainda bem	just as well, so pleased, so relieved
pneu sobresselente	spare tyre
também digo!	I'll say so! I agree!
o único azar	the only piece of bad luck
fronteira	frontier
funcionários	officers
alfândega	Customs
que pouca sorte	what bad luck
graças a Deus	thank God
embraiagem	clutch
afinar os travões	to adjust the brakes (*in Brazil:* **acertar os freios**)
carregar a bateria	to charge the battery
despesa	expense
com que não contávamos	which we did not expect, which we were not counting on
Olha!	Oh look!
vê lá	just imagine
meu Deus	goodness me, my God
como o tempo voa	how time flies
soirée	evening show
peça	play
êxito	success
disponível	available, free

Chapter 10

45 The personal infinitive

The personal infinitive is an inflected infinitive which, although it is unique to Portuguese, need not worry the student, for whom it simplifies syntax. In some cases, for instance, it can replace the more complicated subjunctive.

The formation of the personal infinitive is the same for all verbs, without exception. It is an infinitive with personal endings to indicate the person to whom the infinitive refers. It has only one set of endings, whether the verb is regular or irregular, and it can be used with subject pronouns.

The personal infinitive

	SINGULAR	PLURAL
1st person	**eu** falar	falar**mos**
2nd person (familiar)	falar**es**	falar**em**
2nd person (informal)	**você** falar	
3rd person	**ele/ela** falar	falar**em**

Uses of the personal infinitive

1 in place of the subjunctive

The personal infinitive can replace the subjunctive after verbs of commanding, requesting and emotion, provided that the conjunction is replaced with a preposition. (See *Uses of the subjunctive mood* in section 40.)

In the conjunctions **antes que** and **depois que**, the **que** is replaced with the preposition **de**. (This does <u>not</u> apply to the conjunctions **contanto que, embora que, mesmo que, ainda que, se bem que, logo que, a não que**, all of which need to use the subjunctive.)

subjunctive:	**Ela pediu para que lhe telefonássemos.**
pers inf:	**Ela pediu para lhe telefonarmos.**
	She asked us to telephone him.
subjunctive:	**Vou sair antes que chova.**
pers inf:	**Vou sair antes de chover.**
	I am going out before it rains.

The personal infinitive can also replace the subjunctive in impersonal expressions and after such verbs as **surpreender, agradar, estranhar, ter pena, lamentar, recear**. In these cases, it requires no preposition:

subjunctive:	**É pena que não estejam aqui.**
pers inf:	**É pena não estarem aqui.**
	It's a shame they are not here.
subjunctive:	**É bom que eles vão dar uma volta.**
pers inf:	**E bom irem dar uma volta.**
	It's a good idea for them to go for a walk.

The personal infinitive can replace the subjunctive in adverbial clauses. For example:

subjunctive:	**Partiram sem que lhes disséssemos adeus.**
pers inf:	**Partiram sem lhes dizermos adeus.**
	They left without our saying goodbye to them
subjunctive:	**Não te perdoo até que tu me peças perdão.**
pers inf:	**Não te perdoo até tu me pedires perdão.**
	I am not forgiving you until you apologise.

Notice that in the above examples, subordinate clauses containing a subjunctive are always introduced by **que**, whereas those containing a personal infinitive are not.

3 To express 'on doing something'

The personal infinitive is a simple and convenient way of expressing the English construction 'on' + *present participle*. It can be used in combination with past, present and future tenses. For example:

Ao chegarem, encontraram-se logo com o Primeiro Ministro.
　　On arriving, they met the Prime Minister at once.

In English, to avoid ambiguity, we would probably say, 'On their arrival . . . '. But in Portuguese, the ending **em** immediately identifies 'them' as the subject of the personal infinitive. More examples:

Ao entrarmos, vimos o ladrão.
　　On entering (as we entered / when we went in), we saw the thief.
Só saberei a resposta ao chegar ao escritório.
　　I shall only know the answer on my arriving at the office.

Note: Do not use subject pronouns after **ao** + personal infinitive.

4 To express the reason for doing something, with **por**

The personal infinitive is useful as a succinct way of replacing **porque** + *indicative* as the following examples illustrate.

indicative:	**Não te escrevemos porque não sabíamos a tua morada.**
pers inf.	**Não te escrevemos por não sabermos a tua morada.**
	We did not write to you because we did not know your address.

indicative: **Inácio partiu porque chegou a sua sogra.**
pers inf: **Inácio partiu por chegar a sua sogra.**
Ignatius departed because his mother-in-law
arrived.

5 Idiomatic use to express irony, sarcasm or incredulity

When the personal infinitive is used in this way, the meaning – in speech, at any rate – is likely to be conveyed as
much by intonation as by the construction and form of verb.
Such expressions can often be translated word for word into
English, but are usually best rendered by the use of an extra
phrase. Consider these examples:

Tu, estudares?
You? Studying? *(or:* What? You're actually studying?)
Nós, mentirmos por causa de você?
Us? Tell lies on your account? *(or: Do* you really expect
us to tell lies for your sake?)

Exercise 30

Translate the following:
1 Este livro é para lermos.
2 Não quero comprar o carro sem tu concordares.
3 É pena não poderes vir no próximo domingo.
4 Foi bom trazerem os vossos casacos porque vai estar frio.
5 Receio estarem zangados comigo.
6 Não vieram por estarem cansados.
7 Foi impossível irmos à tourada.
8 Vocês, ganharem a taça mundial?
9 They are going to leave before we arrive.
10 It was impossible for us to see the minister.
11 It surprises me your *(familiar)* saying a thing like that.
12 I said goodbye to them before they left.
13 I cannot give an opinion until we know everything.
14 We didn't have lunch because we did not have time.

Vocabulary

concordar	to agree
casaco	coat
recear	to fear
zangado	cross, angry
tourada	bullfight
taça mundial	World Cup (*In Brazil:* **copa do mundo**)
uma coisa assim/	
uma coisa destas	a thing like that

46 The present participle

The present participle, also known as the gerund, is formed by removing the **r** from the infinitive and adding **ndo** to the stem. There are no exceptions.

fala|r→fala**ndo**	speaking
come|r→come**ndo**	eating
abri|r→abri**ndo**	opening

In general, the use of the present participle in Portuguese is much more limited than in English. It cannot be used as a noun. It is used principally in adverbial clauses.
For example:

Lá continuaram a sua viagem, passando por aldeias, atravessando rios e subindo montanhas.
> There they continued their journey, passing through villages, crossing rivers and ascending mountains.

The Portuguese present participle can be used to translate 'on' + *present participle* in English only when the action described by the present participle precedes the action of the verb in the main clause, or when the two actions are simultaneous. For example:

Dizendo isto, desapareceu.
> On saying this, he disappeared. (So saying, he
> disappeared.)

Sendo assim, aceito com prazer.
> This being the case, I will accept with pleasure.

47 Uses of the infinitive

There are some important instances in Portuguese where the infinitive must be used to translate the English present participle.

1 Continuous tenses

In Portuguese, continuous actions are not expressed by the present participle, as they are in English. Instead, the infinitive is used with the appropriate form of **estar a.** Thus we have:

Estou a ler o jornal. I am reading the paper.
Estavam a jogar futebol. They were playing football.

However, when the action takes place over a prolonged period, it is preferable to use **andar a** + *infinitive* instead of **estar a.** For example:

Ando a aprender português.
> I am learning Portuguese. (I have been learning
> Portuguese.)

Andam a construir uma nova câmara municipal.
> They are building a new town hall.

It is also common in Portuguese to use the simple present and imperfect tenses to express continuous action in the present and past respectively. For example:

Aonde vais? Where are you going?
Que fazias? What were you doing?

In Brazilian Portuguese, however, the present participle is used in continuous tenses. Thus it follows the English pattern exactly:

Eles estão jogando futebol. They are playing football.

2 In place of the gerund

In English, when a verb is used as a noun (the gerund), it is the present participle that is used. In Portuguese it is the infinitive that performs this function. For example:

É proibido fumar. No smoking allowed.

PRACTISE!

Exercise P.10

Please fill in the blanks with the appropriate verbal forms (indicated after). When the subject pronoun is shown after the verbal form, this indicates that the personal infinitive is required. Answers are given in the Key.

Querida amiga Antónia,

Recebi a sua estimada carta há já um mês e ___ [sentir-se] muito envergonhada por não lhe ter ___ [escrever, *past part.*] ainda.

Acredite que não ___ [ser] falta de amizade ou indiferença, mas falta de tempo. Tudo ___ [parecer] ter ___ [conspirar, *past part.*] para que eu não ___ [ter] um minuto de vagar. Tenho ___ [ter] pessoas de família em minha casa, uma delas, doente. Ao mesmo tempo, as obras na minha casa ___ [começar]. E já não ___ [ser, *imp.*] sem tempo! Em face disto tudo acho que você ___ [ir] desculpar-me.

Como ___ [estar] vocês? Como ___ [estar] o tempo aí? Já ___ [eu, saber] que tem ___ [chover, *past part.*] muito no Algarve. Ainda bem! Oxalá chova mais, pois vocês ___ [sofrer] uma prolongada seca, no ano passado, a qual ___ [deverl ter ___ [causar, *past part.*] grande prejuízo à agricultura. Quando me ___ [lembrar] da boa fruta e legumes que eu ___ [comer] nessa paradisíaca região! Aqui tem ___ [chover, *past part.*] muito, ___ [eu, estar] farta de chuva. Se nós ___ [poderl exportar chuva para o vosso país, ___ [estar, *cond.*] mais ricos e vocês em melhor situação ___ [ficar, *cond.*].

___ [Eu, agradecer] -lhe muito o seu convite para ___ [ir, nós] a Portugal para vossa casa. Vocês ___ [ser] muito amáveis mas ___ [eu, crer] que não ___ [irl ser possível porque já ___ [nós, aceitar] o convite que sua irmã nos ___ [fazer] para ___ [passar, nós] o ___ verão de 1998 em Lisboa e ___ [visitar, nós] a EXPO 98 que tanto ___ [nós, querer] ver. Talvez você ___ [poder] ir também. Se vocês ___ [ir], mande-me dizer para ___ [poder, nós] estar lá todos juntos. Espero que ___ [haver] quartos para todos. Deste modo, eu ___ [matar, *imp.*] dois coelhos de uma cajadada. Mas ___ [dizer] me com antecedência porque tenho que marcar as passagens muito antes, senão não ___ [conseguir, *fut.*] ter nenhum lugar.

Bem, por hoje termino. Cá fico aguardando as suas notícias que me ___ [dar] sempre muito prazer, ___ [prometer, *pres. part.*] ser pontual para próxima vez, envio beijinhos aos seus filhos, uma festinha ao cão, cujo nome não me ___ [recordar], um abraço à sua mãe, cumprimentos ao seu marido e, para si muitas saudades desta sua amiga muito grata.

Mariana

envergonhada	ashamed, embarrassed
amizade (*f*)	friendship
vagar	(leisure) time (to spare)
obras (na casa)	building work
Já não era sem tempo!	About time too!
prolongada seca	long drought
prejuízo	loss, damage

legumes *(m pl)*	vegetables
paradisíaco/a	paradise-like
farta de	fed up with
agradecer	to thank
juntos	together
matar dois coelhos de uma cajadada	to kill two birds with one stone
com antecedência	in advance, beforehand
marcar as passagens	to book the flights
senão	otherwise
cá fico aguardando	I shall remain awaiting
festinha	a pat, caress
saudades	love *(as a closing formula in a letter)*

48 'Por' and 'para'

The prepositions **por** and **para** are both used to translate the English 'for' in various situations. Although the general uses given below help to distinguish between uses of **por** and **para,** they are not always easy to apply. It is important, therefore, to observe carefully how they are used in individual cases and to memorise them when the distinction is not clear.

*Uses of **por**, 'for'*

1 On behalf of . . . , on account of . . .

Eu pago a conta por você.
> I will pay the bill for you. (on your behalf)

Ele lutou por ti.
> He fought for you. (on your behalf, *or* on your account)

2 In exchange for . . .

Troco este casaco pelo seu chapéu.
> I will give you this coat for your hat.

3 In expressions of time

Por is used in a number of expressions of time, mainly relating to duration or frequency. When it relates to frequency, it corresponds exactly to the use of 'per' in English:

Eles vieram por duas semanas.
> They came for two weeks. (duration)

Ele vai a Paris duas vezes por semana.
> He goes to Paris twice a week. (frequency)

Pela primeira vez, vi que ela era bonita.
> For the first time, I noticed that she was pretty.

4 Por meaning 'by', 'through', 'along' etc

In most contexts, 'by' is translated by **por**. It is also used to translate 'through' and 'along', especially with verbs of motion. It is frequently used in conjunction with other adverbs to imply motion. For example:

Vou pela praia.
> I am going along the beach.

Viajo a Portugal por França.
> I travel to Portugal through France.

Vamos pela TAP, naturalmente.
> We are going by TAP,* of course.

(* Transportes Aéreos Portugueses – Air Portugal)

É por aqui ou por ali?
> Is it this way or that way?

Por onde desapareceu?
> Where did it disappear to?

Uses of *para*, 'to', 'for'

1 Destination, purpose

In this case, **para** is used mainly with verbs of motion and in expressions where giving or sending is implied. Thus:

Ele vai para o Brasil. He is going to Brazil.
(The preposition **a** also means 'to' but usually implies that the visit will be of short duration, whereas **para** implies a longer or permanent stay.)

Estas flores são para ti.
>These flowers are for you.

Para que faz você isso?
>What are you doing that for?

2 Expressions of fixed time

Whereas **por** is used to express duration ('time within which . . .') or frequency, **para** refers to 'time at which . . .':

Tenho hora marcada para as três.
>I have an appointment for three o'clock.

3 Imminence 'about'

Os pais dele estão para chegar.
>His parents are about to arrive.

Estava para comprar um carro alemão, mas mudei de ideias.
>I was about to buy a German car, but changed my mind.

4 Viewpoint

Esse trabalho é muito difícil para mim.
>This work is very difficult for me.

Este casaco é demasiado grande para ele.
>This coat is too big for him.

49 The prepositions 'a' and 'para'

As we have seen in our second chapter, **a** means 'at' and 'to'. **Para**, apart from its other interpretations, also means 'to'. When we speak of destination, **para** expresses permanency or a longer duration than **a**. For example, when going to work in the morning or returning from it at the end of the day, you'd say:

Vou para o escritório.
>I'm going to the office.

Vou para casa.
>I'm going home.

But if you were only dropping into the office or home for a fleeting visit, you'd say:

Vou ao escritório buscar a correspondência.
  I'm going to the office to get my mail.
Vou a casa buscar as chaves.
  I'm going to my house to get the keys.

Similarly:

Ela vai para o Brasil trabalhar.
  She is going to Brazil to work.
Vamos a Paris passar o fim de semana.
  We are going to Paris to spend the weekend.

50 The definite article

In previous chapters we have seen that in Portuguese, unlike English, the definite article is required before possessive adjectives. For example:

a minha irmã my sister

However, when the relationship between the possessor and the thing possessed is unmistakably clear – such is the case with parts of the body or personal clothing – the possessive adjective is omitted altogether and only the definite article is used. For example:

O meu pai abanou a cabeça.
  My father shook his head.
O homem tirou o chapéu.
  The man took off his hat.

There are a number of occasions when the definite article is used in Portuguese but not in English. The most common of these are listed below.

Names of people: **a Rita, o José** etc

Continents: **a Europa, a Africa** etc

Provinces: **a Estremadura** (south-west Portugal)

Countries: **a Inglaterra** (But Portugal and her former overseas colonies do not require the definite article.)

Cities do not require the article unless they have a physical meaning, as in **o Porto**.

Rivers: **o Tejo** the Tagus, **o Tamisa** the Thames, **o Sena** the Seine.

The definite article is used before **Senhor, Senhora** and **Menina** except in correspondence – in addressing an envelope for example.

In generic expressions: When referring to a class of persons or things in general, the definite article is used. For example:

Os homens cada vez estão mais fracos.
    Men (in general) are getting weaker and weaker.
Os cães ladram.
    Dogs (in general) bark.

In expressions of time, in combination with the prepositions **em** and **a**:

na quarta-feira passada last Wednesday
no inverno in winter
as três horas at three o'clock

Exercise 31

Translate the following.

1 Não tenho tempo para escrever cartas.
2 A Sra. (senhora) D. (dona) Amélia vai ao médico na quarta-feira.
3 A minha irmã vai para o hospital na terça-feira para fazer uma operação à garganta.
4 Digo-lhe isto para seu bem.
5 Não foi por querer que o magoei.
6 No mês passado fui a Paris visitar a minha tia.
7 Muito obrigado pela sua amabilidade.
8 Por mim não me importo.
9 I have no news for you. *(familiar)*
10 He fought for the rights of Mankind.
11 He has gone to London on business.
12 Are you *(formal)* going home now?
13 Anthony went to Africa to work.
14 I beg your pardon for arriving late.
15 I am going to bed.

Vocabulary

garganta	throat
por querer	on purpose
magoar	to hurt
não me importo	I don't mind

CONVERSATION

Acidentes e incidentes/Accidents and incidents

1 *Catástrofes domésticas*

a Sra. A. Hoje tem sido um daqueles dias de azar. O meu autoclismo recusa-se a funcionar, o cano do lava-louças está entupido e a torneira da banheira continua a pingar sem cessar.

a Sra. B. Você tem de chamar um canalizador.

a Sra. A. Sim, e não é só ele. A campaínha da porta não toca, não sei porquê. A televisão está avariada e os electricistas estão em greve. A minha mulher a dias não está em greve mas fez gazeta hoje, dizendo que tinha uma grande constipação. E amanhã tenho estes convidados que chegam de Londres para virem passar uma semana connosco. Valha-me Deus! Que vou fazer?

a Sra. B. Coitada! Mas não se apoquente desse modo porque não remedeia nada. Eu aconselhava-a a que recebesse os seus convidados muito calmamente e que lhes apresentasse a situaçao duma maneira cómica. Diga-lhes que o ambiente é primitivo. Os ingleses têm um extraordinário sentido de humor e apreciam muito as pessoas que fazem brincadeira de tudo quanto é aborrecido.

2 *Fogo*

1º homen Socorro! Socorro! Chamem os bombeiros e a
ambulância.

2º homen O que é? Onde é o incêndio?

1º homen É ali no mato, está-se a alastrar rapidamente. E
oiço crianças a chorarem e pessoas a gritarem.
Devem ser famílias que foram lá hoje fazer
piquenique. Com um dia tão lindo! E é por
isso que as labaredas avançam rapidamente
porque está tudo tão seco! Oxalá não haja
mortos ou ferimentos graves.

2º homen Se Deus quiser não haverá. Olhe, cá estão as
ambulâncias e os bombeiros. Levaram só dois
minutos. São muito competentes!

1º homen Que pena o mato ficar queimado! Tinha
árvores tão antigas e magestosas!

2º homen Possivelmente foi um irresponsável que atirou
o cigarro para o chão, sem pensar nas
consequências.

3 *Uma anedota – a joke*

No comboio, um passageiro viu um outro cuspir no
chão. Muito chocado com esta acção imprópria, ele
decidiu dizer ao outro:

> – O senhor não leu o aviso na parede que diz
> 'É proibido aos senhores passageiros cuspirem
> no chão'?

> – Sim, li. Mas eu não sou passageiro, sou
> empregado da carris.

Vocabulary

1

azar	bad luck
autoclismo	the flush (*of the cistern*)
o cano do lava-louças	the pipe of the sink
entupido	blocked
a torneira	the tap
banheira	the bathtub
pingar	to drip, dripping
canalizador	plumber (*in Brazil:* bombeiro, tanoeiro)
campainha da porta	the door bell
tocar	to ring (*also* to play music)
A televisão está avariada.	The TV is out of order.
em greve	on strike
mulher a dias	daily woman, charlady
Fez gazeta hoje.	She has not turned up today.
uma grande constipação	a nasty cold
convidados	guests
Valha-me Deus.	May God help me.
Coitada!	Poor you!
Não se apoquente desse modo.	Don't worry yourself like that. Don't upset yourself in this way.
Não remedeia.	It does not help. It does not solve anything.
aconselhava	I would advise
ambiente	environment
sentido de humor	sense of humour
fazer brincadeira de	to make fun of

2

Socorro!	Help!
bombeiros	firemen
incêndio	fire
mato	woods, undergrowth, scrub
alastrar-se	to spread
oiço	I hear

chorar	to cry
gritar	to shout, to scream
labaredas	flames
avançar	to advance
seco	dry
mortos	dead people *(in this case* deaths)
ferimentos graves	serious injuries
se Deus quiser	God willing
Olhe!	Look!
competente	efficient
Que pena!	What a shame!
queimado	burnt
atirar	to throw
cigarro	cigarette
chão *(m)*	floor, ground

3

cuspir	to spit
aviso	notice
parede *(f)*	wall
empregado	
da carris	railway employee

Reading practice

A menina do mar

—Eu sou uma menina do mar. Chamo-me Menina do Mar e não tenho outro nome. Não sei onde nasci. Um dia uma gaivota trouxe-me no bico para esta praia. Pôs-me numa rocha na maré vaza e o polvo, o caranguejo e o peixe tomaram conta de mim. Vivemos os quatro numa gruta muito bonita. O polvo arruma a casa, alisa a areia, vai buscar a comida. É de nós todos o que trabalha mais, porque tem muitos braços. O caranguejo é o cozinheiro. Faz caldo verde com limos, sorvetes de espuma, e salada de algas, sopa de tartaruga, caviar e muitas outras receitas. É um grande cozinheiro. Quando a comida está pronta o polvo põe a mesa. A toalha é uma alga branca e os pratos são conchas. Depois, à noite, o polvo faz a minha cama com algas muito verdes e muito macias. Mas o costureiro dos meus vestidos é o caranguejo. E é também o meu ourives: ele é que faz os meus colares de búzios, de corais e de pérolas. O peixe não faz nada porque não tem mãos, nem braços com ventosas como o polvo, nem braços com tenazes como o caranguejo. Só tem barbatanas e as barbatanas servem só para nadar. Mas é o meu melhor amigo. Como não tem braços nunca me põe de castigo. É com ele que eu brinco. Quando a maré está vazia brincamos nas rochas; quando está maré alta damos passeios no fundo do mar. Tu nunca foste ao fundo do mar e não sabes como lá tudo é bonito. Há florestas de algas jardins de anémonas, prados de conchas. Há cavalos marinhos suspensos na água com um ar espantado, como pontos de interrogação. Há flores que parecem animais e animais que parecem flores. Há grutas misteriosas azuis-escuras, roxas, verdes e há planícies sem fim de areia fina, branca e lisa. Tu és da terra e se fosses ao fundo do mar morrias afogado. Mas eu sou uma menina do mar. Posso respirar dentro da água como os peixes e posso respirar fora da água como os homens.

—E agora que já contei a minha história leva-me outra vez para o pé dos meus amigos que devem estar aflitíssimos.

O rapaz pegou na Menina do Mar com muito cuidado na palma da mão e levou-a outra vez para o sítio de onde a tinha trazido. O polvo, o caranguejo e o peixe – lá estavam os três a chorar abraçados.

—Estou aqui—gritou a menina do mar.

Taken and abridged from *A Menina do Mar* by Sofia de Melo Breyner, one of the best-known writers of modern Portuguese narrative.

The little girl of the sea

'I am a little girl of the sea. My name is Little Girl of the Sea and I do not have any other name. I don't know where I was born. One day a seagull brought me in its beak to this beach. It put me down on a rock at low tide and the octopus, the crab and the fish took care of me. The four of us live in a beautiful cave. The octopus tidies the house up, smooths the sand and fetches food. He works more than any of us because he has many arms. The crab is the cook. He makes green broth with seaweed, foam ice-cream and algae salad, turtle soup, caviar and many other recipes. He is a great cook. When the meal is ready, the octopus sets the table. The table-cloth is a white seaweed and the plates are sea-shells. Later, at night the octopus makes my bed with very soft, very green seaweed. But my dressmaker is the crab. He is also my jeweller: he makes my necklaces out of conch-shells, coral and pearls. The fish does not do anything because he has no hands, nor arms with suckers like the octopus nor arms with pincers as the crab has. He only has fins and the fins are only good for swimming. But he is my best friend. As he does not have any arms he cannot punish me. It is with him that I play. When the tide is out we play on the rocks; when it is high tide we go for strolls on the sea-bed. You have never been to the bottom of the sea and so you have no idea how beautiful everything is there. There are forests of seaweed, gardens of sea-anemones, fields of shells. There are sea-horses hanging in the water, looking perplexed like question marks. There are flowers which look like animals and animals which seem to be flowers. There are mysterious grottos - dark blue, purple, green - and there are endless plains with soft, smooth, white sand. You come from the land and if you went to the bottom of the sea you would drown. But I am a little girl of the sea. I can breathe under the water as the fish do, and out of it like men.

'And now that I have told you my story, please take me back to my friends who must be extremely worried.'

The boy picked the Little Girl of the Sea up very carefully in the palm of his hand, and took her back to the place from which he had brought her. The octopus, the crab and the fish - there they were, the three of them crying in each other's arms.

'I am here' shouted the little girl of the sea.

Translated from the original by Maria Fernanda Allen.

Dos jornais . . .

Dois cadastrados fugiram do tribunal

Um distúrbio simulado por um detido e sua mulher, no momento em que este se preparava para ser julgado no Tribunal de Paços de Ferreira, veio permitir a sua fuga juntamente com outro detido.

O insólito caso, segundo o «DN» apurou, deu-se na terça--feira, quando Casimiro da Silva de 31 anos, a cumprir uma pena de sete anos na Penitenciária de Coimbra, se preparava para ser julgado no referido tribunal por ter agredido, há cerca de um ano, um guarda prisional na Cadeia Central do Norte.

No mesmo dia, o Tribunal de Paços de Ferreira iria tambem julgar Jaime da Silva de 26 anos, preso em Custóias sob a acusação de ter assaltado uma residência e roubado jóias avaliadas em 400 contos.

Na altura em que o Casimiro aguardava numa sala contígua à sala de audiências o início do julgamento, apareceu a sua mulher, tendo-se estabelecido imediatamente uma cena violenta entre os dois. Aí, os guardas intervieram a separá--los e decidiram encerrar o Casimiro numa cela onde também se encontrava o outro réu.

Pouco depois quando os guardas se dirigiram à cela para trazerem o Casimiro até à sala de audiências, deparou-se--lhes a porta arrombada. Dos detidos nem sinal. No chão, segundo o depoimento dos guardas, encontrava-se abandonado um pé-de-cabra, ferramenta que, no meio da altercação, deve ter sido passada ao Casimiro por sua mulher.

Esta eficiente evasão só não causou grande espanto por Casimiro ser um «especialista» neste domínio. O seu cadastro regista uma série de fugas tal como aconteceu em Custóias, quando saltou o muro da prisão e fugiu no seu próprio automóvel.

From the newspapers . . .

Two men with prison records escaped from court

A man held in custody, and his wife, faked a disturbance just before his case was due to be heard at the court of Paços de Ferreira, which enabled him to escape together with another detained man.

The unusual occurrence, according to Diario de Noticias, took place on Tuesday when Casimiro da Silva, 31 years old, serving a sentence of seven years at Coimbra prison, was about to be tried in the above-mentioned court for assaulting a prison warder in the Central Northern prison, about a year ago.

The same day, the court at Paços de Ferreira was also going to hear the case of Jaime da Silva, 26 years old, apprehended in Custoais and accused of having broken into a home and stolen jewels worth 400,000 escudos.

While Casimiro waited in a room adjacent to the courtroom for his case to be heard, his wife came in and at once started a violent scene. The guards intervened and decided to lock Casimiro up in a cell already occupied by the other accused.

A little while afterwards, when the warders went to the cell to take Casimiro to the courtroom, they saw the door broken open. Of the detainees - no sign. On the floor, according to the testimony of the warders, there was a crowbar lying abandoned, a tool which must have been passed to Casimiro by his wife during the altercation.

This very efficient escape did not cause great surprise, because Casimiro is already known as a "specialist" in this field. His record shows a series of escapes, like the one which happened in Custoias when he jumped the prison wall and got away in his own car.

From *Diario de Noticias*
translated by Maria Fernanda Allen.

Portugal e Brasil

Nós brasileiros, melhor do que ninguém, podemos falar sobre Portugal e os portuguêses. Pois é verdade que no tempo das suas descobertas os navegadores portuguêses foram donos de terras em todos os continentes; mas foi no Brasil que ficou realmente a marca do gênio português. Eram eles um povo pequeno, que vivia num pequeno país. E assim mesmo tomaram posse do nosso imenso território e o povoaram. Deram-nos a sua lingua, os seus costumes e a sua religião. Lutavam às vezes com os índios, mas preferiam conviver em paz com eles, juntos fundando novas famílias, povoações e cidades.

Na verdade nós somos o que o português nos fêz. No século passado, quando começaram a chegar ao Brasil as grandes ondas de emigrantes italianos, alemães, árabes, etc., os portuguêses já estavam aqui trabalhando sòzinhos há mais de trezentos anos. O Brasil já tinha então a sua nacionalidade própria, e não mudou mais. Os recém-chegados é que mudaram e foram assimilados.

Fiéis à nossa formação pacífica, somos um povo pacífico. Fizemos a independência, a abolição da escravatura, a república, sem guerra; e fazemos as nossas revoluçoes quase sem luta ou sem derramar sangue de irmãos. Procurando vencer as dificuldades por meio de entendimentos e não lutando. E podemos dizer que esse amor à compreensão e à paz é a melhor herança que Portugal nos deixou.

From *Modern Portuguese* published in the United States by Alfred A. Knopf Inc., New York and distributed by Random House Inc., New York

Portugal and Brazil

We the Brazilians, better than anyone else, can speak about Portugal and the Portuguese. It is a fact that in the days of maritime exploration the Portuguese navigators were masters of lands in all the continents; but it was really in Brazil that the Portuguese left the mark of their genius.

They were a small nation who lived in a small country. But they took possession of our immense territory and they populated it. They gave us their language, their customs and their religion. Sometimes they fought with the native Indians but they preferred to live in peace with them, together founding new families, villages and cities.

Indeed, we are what the Portuguese made us. Last century, when the great waves of Italian, German and Arab emigrants began to arrive in Brazil, the Portuguese had already been working alone in Brazil for more than three hundred years. Brazil had by then her own identity which stayed the same. It was the newcomers who changed and were assimilated.

Faithful to our peaceful formation, we are a peaceful people. We got our independence, abolished slavery, founded our republic without wars; and we made our revolutions almost without fighting and without spilling our brethren's blood. We try to overcome our difficulties by means of understanding and not conflict. And we can say that this love of understanding and of peace is the best legacy Portugal left us.

Translated by Maria Fernanda Allen.

A cozinha portuguesa

A cozinha portuguesa é bem conhecida pela sua rica variedade, com pratos típicos para cada região. Embora não seja tão sofisticada como a francesa é, no entanto, muito saborosa e saudável. É também bastante diferente das outras cuilnárias europeias.

Para os portugueses comer é o maior prazer na vida. Esta predilecção por boa comida reflete-se em inumeráveis expressões populares como, por exemplo: 'ficou tudo em águas de bacalhau'. Na hora das refeições, se alguém por acaso chegar é logo convidado a comer com um "É servido/a?" Normalmente, a resposta é: "Não. muito obrigado. Bom proveito!"

Falar da cozinha portuguesa é falar de tomate, o qual se põe em saladas — tanto em mixta como por si só com um pouco de cebola e salsa — sopa, caçarolas e no refugado para se fazer o famoso guisado. Até há uma compota de tomate; geralmente, feita em casa. Os outros ingredientes são: a cebola, o alho, a folha de louro, o limão, o vinho branco ou tinto, muita salsa e coentros e, não devemos esquecer, o 'piri-piri' agora à venda nos supermercados ingleses.

Quanto à sobremesa, os portugueses normalmente preferem fruta embora haja doces e pudins de fazer crescer água na boca. Estes são consumidos principalmente em dias de festa quando ignoramos dietas e conselhos sensatos sobre a saúde. Não há pudim ou doce que não se faça com ovos, muitos ovos, e açucar. Em contrapartida, usa-se pouca farinha. A canela, quer em pó quer em pau, é um ingrediente indispensável nestes doces e pudins, assim como bolos e frituras. Os outros igualmente essenciais são: Vinho do Porto, laranjas limões, amêndoas e nozes.

Porém, o português não pode resistir aos pastéis e bolos com o seu chá ou café e os mais populares são os pastéis de nata ou pastéis de Belém os quais, de preferência, devem ser comidos quentes (tal como fazem na Pastelaria Belém) e pulvilhados de canela. Há inumeráveis pastelarias por todo o país exibindo uma grande variedade de pastéis e bolos únicos, que tentam até mesmo o mais forte.

Começa-se uma refeição quase sempre por uma sopa. Creio que não há outro país com tantas sopas diferentes. A mais conhecida é o Caldo Verde. Depois temos a canja, a sopa de feijão, de grão, sopa de ossos, de carne, de coentros de pão, de massa, de peixe, de legumes, etc.

O prato tradicional português é o bacalhau. Há mais de duzentas receitas de bacalhau de acordo com uns e mais de mil segundo outros. O número varia conforme o número de copos de vinho que se bebeu durante um grande e suculento jantar português.

Portuguese cuisine

Portuguese cuisine is known for its rich variety, with typical dishes for each region. Although it is not as sophisticated as French cuisine, it is, nevertheless, very tasty and healthy. It is also quite distinct from other European cuisines.

The Portuguese enjoy eating: for them, it is the greatest pleasure in life. Their love for good food is reflected in numerous popular expressions such as: "it all came to nothing (*lit.* like cod's water)". At meal times, if anyone should, by chance, drop by, he/she is invited with: "Would you like to partake? (*lit.* would you like to be served?)". Usually, the reply is: "No, thank you. Enjoy your meal!"

When one speaks of Portuguese food, one is speaking of tomatoes. You find them in salads – both in mixed as well as on their own with a touch of onion and parsley – in soup, casseroles and in the 'refogado' [fried onions] which is the first step for the famous 'guisado' (a kind of stew). There is even a home-made tomato jam. The other ingredients of Portuguese cuisine are: onions, garlic, bay leaf, lemon, white or red wine, a lot of parsley and coriander, and we shouldn't forget the 'piri-piri', which is now available in British supermarkets.

As for dessert, Portuguese people normally prefer to eat fruit though they have a great assortment of puddings and sweets which make one's mouth water. These are eaten especially at parties and celebrations when one ignores diets and sensible advice on health. No pudding or sweet is made without eggs, many eggs, and sugar. On the other hand, they don't use much flour. Cinnamon, whether in powder or stick, is an indispensable ingredient in these sweets and puddings, as well as cakes and sweet fritters. The other vital items are Port wine, oranges, almonds and nuts.

However, the Portuguese cannot resist eating pastries with tea or coffee, and the most popular of all are the 'cream or Belem tarts' which, ideally, should be eaten hot (as they do in the Belem Patisserie) and sprinkled with cinnamon. There are numerous pastry-shops all over Portugal, displaying a great variety of unique pastries and cakes ready to tempt even the strongest.

A Portuguese meal invariably starts with soup. I believe there is no other country with so many different soups. The best known one is 'Green Broth', followed by 'chicken broth', bean soup, chick-pea, bones, onion, meat, coriander, bread, pasta, fish, vegetable soup, etc.

The Portuguese traditional dish is dried cod. There are more than 200 recipes, according to some and 1000 according to others. The number varies depending on the number of glasses of wine you have consumed during a hearty and succulent Portuguese dinner.

Santo António, padroeiro de Lisboa

Santo António de Lisboa, também conhecido por Santo António de Pádua, nasceu em Lisboa a 15 de agosto de 1195. Filho de pais nobres, o seu primeiro nome foi Fernando de Bulhões.

Estudou as suas primeiras letras na Catedral de Lisboa, depois no Mosteiro de São Vicente, Lisboa, e no Mosteiro de Santa Cruz de Coimbra (um centro de cultura), ingressando, mais tarde, na ordem de São Francisco onde tomou o nome de Frei António.

Frei António era muito bondoso e humilde apesar de possuir o dom da palavra e de ser um homem de grande saber. Estas qualidades tornaram-se célebres na Itália onde pregava e, a pedido de São Francisco de Assis, ensinava Teologia. O próprio Papa ficou maravilhado ao ouvir um sermão dele.

Foi o acaso que o levou a Itália quando, vindo de Marrocos onde tinha ido pregar a sua fé cristã, o seu barco deu às costas de Sicília, devido a uma grande tempestade.

A 13 de junho de 1231, quando residia em Pádua, Frei António entregou a sua alma a Deus, com trinta e seis anos incompletos.

Todos os anos, nesta data, celebra-se em Lisboa - e mesmo por todo o país - o dia, ou melhor, a noite de Santo António. Realizam-se festas e a alegria reina por toda a parte. Há cantigas e marchas pelas ruas de Lisboa; sardinhas assadas e vinho até altas horas. Nas janelas vêem-se os vasos com mangericos e um cravo de papel vermelho espetado em cada um deles. É o dia dos namorados e de se pedir namoro, pois Santo António é o protector das moças solteiras.

De religioso, não há nada nestas festas as quais, juntamente com a festa de São João e a de São Pedro respectivamente no dia 24 e 29 do mesmo mês, têm o nome de Festas Populares.

[*M. F. Allen*]

Saint Anthony – Lisbon's patron saint

Saint Anthony of Lisbon, also known as St Anthony of Padua, was born in Lisbon on 15th August 1195. Son of noble parents, his original name was Fernando de Bulhões.

He studied at Lisbon Cathedral, St Vincent's Church in Lisbon, Santa Cruz Monastery in Coimbra (a seat of learning), and went on to join the Order of St Francis where he took the name of Friar Anthony.

Friar Anthony was very kind and humble despite being a brilliant speaker [*lit.* having a talent for speech] and a scholar. He was renowned for these qualities and gifts throughout Italy, where he was preaching and also, at the request of St Francis, teaching theology. The Pope himself stood in wonder when he listened to one of his sermons.

Chance had taken him to Italy when his boat, in which he was returning from preaching in Morocco, ended up in Sicily after a violent storm.

On 13th June 1231, when he was living in Padua, Friar Anthony departed this life [*lit.* gave his soul to God]. He was not quite 36 years old.

Every year, this date is celebrated in Lisbon - in fact throughout the country - as St Anthony's Day, or rather, St Anthony's Night. Festivities take place and merrymaking reigns everywhere. There are songs and 'marchas' [traditional Lisbon dances as they parade] through Lisbon's streets, charcoal-grilled sardines and wine far into the night. On the window-sills one can see flower pots with 'mangericos' [a kind of sweet basil grown for its aroma and decorative purposes around this time] and a red paper carnation stuck in each of them. This is the day for lovers and the day when boy asks girl to go out with him, for St Anthony is the protector of single girls.

There is nothing religious about these festivities which, together with St John's and St Peter's Days, respectively on 24th and 29th June, have the name of Popular Festivities.

Letters

Here is some guidance on how to begin and end correspondence, followed by a model business letter. Refer also to the personal letter in Chapter 10's *Practice!* section.

The date is generally prefaced by the name of the place the sender is writing from: **Londres, 9 de setembro de 1996.** (Remember that the months in Portuguese now begin with a small letter; this is a comparatively recent change in orthography, and many older people may still use a capital letter.)

1:    If writing to friends or colleagues, begin with **Querido** or **Querida . . .** (Dear . . .), depending of course on the friend's gender; equally, you could start with **Caro/a . . .** :

Querida Natália; Caro Paulo; Querida amiga.

Depending on the degree of familiarity or friendship, carry on with (1a) the familiar verbal form of 'tu' or (1b) of 'você':

1a:
Então como vais? Já viste o Pedro? Dá-lhe um abraço da minha parte. Quando vens a Londres? Já sinto saudades de ti e de Sintra.

> Well, how are things with you? Have you seen Peter? Give him a hug from me. When are you coming to London? I am missing you and Sintra.

1b:
Espero que você esteja bem e o seu marido vá melhor. Quando é que vocês vêm cá?

> I hope you are well and that your husband is better. When are you (*pl*) coming here?

2:    There is another form of address which is neither familiar nor formal, but which is friendly and at the same time courteous. It uses the forename followed by the same verbal form as for 'você'. This style is preferred by those who do not like using 'você':

Cara Rita, Como está? Há quanto tempo que ando para lhe escrever! Infelizmente não tenho tido um momento para o fazer. Eu sei que a Rita vai desculpar-me. Quero agradecer à Rita o seu amável convite para eu ir a Lisboa passar o Carnaval consigo . . .

Dear Rita, How are you? I have been meaning to write to you for so long! Alas, I have not had one moment to do it. I know that you will forgive me. I want to thank you for your kind invitation for me to come to Lisbon and spend Carnival with you . . .

3: In formal or business letters the 'Dear Sir' or 'Dear Madam' formula is expressed by **Exmo. Senhor** or **Exma. Senhora**. If you are writing 'Dear Sirs', put **Exmos. Senhores** or **Amigos e Senhores. Exmo./a.** is an abbreviation of **Excelentíssimo/a**; *in Brazil* the abbreviation is written as **Ilmo./a.**, being short for **Ilustríssimo/a.**

Thereafter in such letters, 'you' is normally translated by **V.Exa.** for **Vossa Excelência** (both genders, singular) and **V.Exas.** in the plural. *(In Brazil:* **V.Sia. (Vossa Senhoria)**, plural **V.Sias.**) Thus:

Acuso a recepção *(or:* **o recebimento) de vossa carta datada 96-3-12, na qual V.Exas. nos perguntavam se nós ainda estávamos interessados em manter relações com a vossa firma . . .**

I acknowledge receipt of your letter dated 12th March 1996, in which you were asking if we were still interested in maintaining our relations with your firm . . .

4: When it comes to ending your letter, the closing formulae (as you'd expect) depend upon how well you know your correspondent. Referring back to the paragraph numbers above:

(1a) **Um grande abraço para ti –** or: **Um beijinho –** or: **Saudades –**

A hug/a kiss for you –, Love –, Missing you –.

(1b, 2) **Abraços para si e seu marido –**

Love [*lit.* embraces, hugs] to you and your husband – or:

Cumprimentos ao seu marido/à sua familia –
Best regards to your husband/to your family –

Saudades, the plural form of that typically Portuguese word for longing, yearning, homesickness, can be used to signify anything from 'love' to 'regards'.

(3) [See next page]

Carta comercial em resposta a uma queixa

Lisboa, 8 de maio de 19_

Exmos. Senhores*
Fonseca & Ca.
Porto

Amigos e Senhores*

Venho acusar a recepção da v/ estimada carta de 17 do mês findo, na qual V. Exas. se queixam da demora na entrega das mercadorias encomendadas pelo vosso favor de 11 de agosto.

Não foi por culpa nossa que elas não foram expedidas, mas devido à greve dos trabalhadores da doca, que durou uns 15 dias. Logo que seja possível darei por telegrama a data do embarque.

Lamentando a inconveniencia que esta demora lhes cause, somos com estima e consideração.

De V. Exas.*
Atenciosamente

Assinatura

* *Alternative forms of address should be noted in this 'Letters' section.*

(3) **Cordiais saudações** – or: **Com estima e consideração, subscrevo-me –**

Best regards or Yours sincerely / Yours faithfully

De V.Exas.	*In Brazil:* **De V.Sias.**
Atenciosamente	**Atentamente**
Yours faithfully	Yours faithfully

Commercial letter in reply to a complaint

Lisbon, 8 May 19_

Messrs Fonseca & Co.
Porto

Dear Sirs,

I acknowledge receipt of your [esteemed] letter of the 17th of last month, in which you have complained about the delay in the delivery of the goods you ordered in your letter of the 11th of August.

It was not through any fault of ours that they were not forwarded, but due to a strike by dock workers, which lasted 15 days. I shall send you a telegram, as soon as possible, giving the date of their despatch.

We very much regret and apologise for the inconvenience this delay may cause you, and await your kind orders in the future.

Yours faithfully,

Signature

Idiomatic expressions

Ones linked to certain verbs:

dar

dar horas   to strike the hour
dar corda ao relógio   to wind (up) the clock/watch
dar baixa ao hospital   to be admitted into hospital (for treatment)
O médico deu-lhe alta.   The doctor discharged him (from the hospital). *See* **ter**
A janela dá para o mar.   The window looks out on the sea.
dar para   to have a flair for (anything)
Ela dá para a música.   She has a flair for music.
O polícia não deu por isso.   The police did not notice it/weren't aware of it/didn't realize it.
dar com   to come across, to bump into (someone)
dar-se bem/mal em . . .   to be well and happy/unhappy in . . . (a place)
dar-se bem mal com . . .   to get along well/badly with . . . (someone)
dar à luz   to give birth
dar por certo   to take for granted
Quem me dera!   How I wish! Would that I might! *(this is the pluperfect tense of* **dar***)*
ao Deus dará   aimlessly (left to one's own fate)
dar uma vista de olhos   to take a quick look at/through

deixar

Ele deixou de fumar.   He stopped smoking.
Deixe-me em paz.   Leave me alone.
Ela deixou as cartas para outro dia.   She put off (writing) the letters until another day.
Elas deixaram as camas por fazer.   They left the beds unmade.

estar

estar para sair   to be on the point of going out
O teatro estava às moscas.   The theatre was *(literally)* left
  to the flies (i.e. without customers).
O cinema estava à cunha.   The cinema was packed.
O trabalho está por fazer.   The work remains undone.
A gasolina está pela hora da morte.   Petrol has become
  very expensive.
estar de boa maré/má maré   to be in a good mood/bad
  mood
estar em dia com . . .   to be up to date with . . .
  (correspondence etc)
estar com fome/sede *(in Brazil:* **sêde)**   to be hungry/thirsty
estar com sono/frio/calor   to be sleepy/hot/cold
estar com sorte/ciúmes/medo *(in Brazil:* **mêdo)**   to be
  lucky/jealous/afraid
estar com pressa/vontade de/razão   to be in a hurry/to
  feel like/to be right

fazer

fazer a barba   to shave oneself
fazer anos   to have a birthday
Ele faz trinta anos hoje.   He is thirty today.
Faz bom/mau tempo.   The weather is good/bad.
Ela só faz asneiras.   She only makes mistakes.
Você fez muito bem/mal.   You did the right/wrong thing.
Nadar faz bem à saúde.   Swimming is good for the health.
fazer as vontades de . . .   to do the will of/to give into the
  wishes of someone
Farei o possível.   I will do my best.
Que é feito dela?   What has happened to her?
fazer-se de bôbo   to play dumb
fazer uma viagem   to take a trip/to go on a journey

ficar

Este chapéu fica-lhe bem.   This hat suits you.
Ele ficou bem no exame.   He passed the exam.
Fica para a semana.   Let us make it (an appointment) next
  week.

Fica para a outra vez.   We'll make it another time.
Fique descansada.   Don't worry, rest assured.
Fico contente.   I am so happy. (in respect of some news
   just learnt)
Isto fica entre nós.   This is between us.
Ele ficou sem dinheiro.   He was left without money.

ir

ir ter com   to go to meet
ir de encontro a   to collide with
ir de avião/de autocarro (*in Brazil:* **omnibus)/de barco** to
   fly/to go by bus/boat
ir a pé/a cavalo to walk, to go on foot/to ride
Vai mal de saúde.   He is in poor health.
   (*Also*: **Está muito mal.**)
Como vão?   How are you (*pl.*)
Ir a Roma e não ver o Papa.   To go Rome and not see the
   Pope (i.e. to go to a place and not see what the place is
   famous for; *or* not to accomplish one's mission or
   purpose.)
Ela vai aos ares.   She hits the ceiling/blows up in a rage.
Vamos!   Let's go!
Sempre foi a Portugal?   Did you go to Portugal (in the
   end/after all)?

pôr

pôr a mesa   to set the table
pôr de castigo   to punish
Ela pô-lo na rua.   She turned him out of doors. (*Literally*
   into the street)
pôr-se a   to begin to
Ela pôs-se a falar muito depressa.   She began to speak
   hurriedly.
O homem põe e Deus dispõe.   Man proposes and God
   disposes.
sem tirar nem pôr   precisely/just like that
o pôr de sol   sunset

querer

se quiser   if you like
como quiser (queira)   as you wish
sem querer   unintentionally
Ela fez por querer.   She did it on purpose.
Queira sentar-se.   Please sit down.
Quem quer vai, quem não quer manda.   If you want a
   thing done, do it yourself.

ser

É isso mesmo.   That's just it.
É sempre assim.   It always happens that way.
Como foi que . . . ?   How did it happen that . . . ?
É por minha conta.   It's on me. (*i.e.* I will pay the bill.)
a não ser que   unless
se eu fosse você . . .   if I were you . . .
Seja como fôr . . .   Be that as it may (in any case).
tal como deve ser   as it should be
É a minha vez.   It is my turn.
o ser humano   the human being

Portuguese equivalents of some
   English idiomatic expressions:

What is it about?   **De que se trata?**
Say no more about it.   **Não fale mais nisso.**
Forget about it.   **Não pense mais nisso.**
ages ago   **há muito tempo**
all at once   **de repente**
all the better   **tanto melhor**
It is all the same to me.   **É-me indiferente./Tanto se me dá.**
as it were/so to speak   **por assim dizer**
as you like   **como quiser**
to back out (of an agreement or commitment)   **faltar ao
   prometido**

Stop beating about the bush. **Deixe-se de rodeios.**

I hope you will soon be better. **Desejo-lhe as melhoras.**

By the way ... **A propósito ...**

How did it come about? **Como aconteceu isso?**

Come on!/Come along!/Let's go! **Vamos!**

to be at ease **pôr-se à vontade/estar à vontade**

Take it easy. **Não se canse.**

to fall asleep **adormecer**

to fall in love **apaixonar-se**

to get dark **escurecer/anoitecer**

It is getting late. **Está a fazer-se tarde** (*in Brazil:* **entardecendo**).

to get the sack **ser despedido**

Get out! **Fora!/Rua!**

How are you getting on? **Como lhe corre a vida?/Como vão as coisas?**

I couldn't get a word in edgeways. **Não consegui abrir a boca./Não abri bico.**

I give in. **Desisto./Dou-me por vencido.**

I give up. **Desisto.**

I am going to get ready. **Vou-me arranjar./Vou-me aprontar.**

going like hot cakes **vendendo-se muito bem**

He is hard up. **Ele está em apuros/sem dinheiro.**

I work hard. **Trabalho muito.**

hard to please **difícil de contentar**

He has hardly said one word. **Ele mal disse uma palavra.**

Help! **Socorro!**

Can't be helped! **Não há remédio!/Que remédio!**

Help yourself! **Sirva-se!**

a long way off **a uma grande distancia**

So long! **Adeus!/Até logo!**

to look after **tomar conta de/olhar por**

to look like **parecer-se com**

to make a mistake **enganar-se**

to make the most of it **tirar o melhor partido**

to make up one's mind **decidir-se a**

Never mind./It does not matter. **Não faz mal./Não tem importância.**

Do you mind? **Importa-se?**

Mind the step! **Cuidado com o degrau!**

Mind your own business.   **Meta-se na sua vida./Isto não
tem nada a ver consigo**.

to be in a good frame of mind/in a good mood   **estar bem
disposto**

She does not mince words.   **Ela não tem papas na língua.**

more or less   **mais ou menos**

to the right   **à direita**

to be right   **ter razão**

It is all right.   **Está bem.**

You haven't the right.   **Não tem o direito.**

right and wrong   **o bem e o mal**

It serves you right!   **É bem feito!**

You don't say!/Don't tell me!   **Não me diga!**

to be out of one's senses   **perder o juizo**

to drive a person out of his senses   **fazer perder a cabeça
a . . .**

It does not make any sense.   **Não faz sentido nenhum.**

so-so   **assim assim**

to take advantage of (to take the opportunity)   **aproveitar-
-se de**

to take (unfair) advantage of   **tirar partido de/abusar**

to take a photograph   **tirar uma fotografia**

to take place   **realizar-se/efectuar-se**

It takes all the fun out of it.   **Tira-lhe a graça toda.**

That's up to you.   **Isso é consigo.**

Where there's a will there's a way.   **Querer é poder.**

against my will   **contra minha vontade**

If God wills it.   **Se Deus quiser.**

It is not worth while.   **Não vale a pena.**

More useful words and phrases

em viagem/travelling

Há uma demora de duas horas.   There is a delay of two hours.

O avião está atrasado.   The plane is late.

devido ao nevoeiro/greve   due to fog/strike

Onde é a alfândega/o Posto de Pronto-Socorro/a saída?   Where is the Customs/the First-Aid Post/the exit?

Tem alguma a coisa a declarar?   Have you anything to declare?

Falta-me uma mala.   One suitcase of mine is missing.

cinto de segurança   safety belt

É proibido fumar.   Smoking not allowed.

Sinto-me enjoado/-a.   I feel air-sick (sea-sick).

Onde são os lavabos/é o toilete/é a retrete?   Where are the lavatories?

A que horas atracou o barco?   What time did the boat arrive?

Os passageiros já estão a desembarcar.   The passengers are already disembarking.

As passagens são caras.   The fares (by boat or plane) are expensive.

bagageiro   porter

no comboio/on the train

Quero dois bilhetes de ida e volta para o Porto.   I want (would like) two return tickets for Oporto.

É preciso marcar os lugares?   Is it necessary to book the seats?

De que linha parte o comboio (*in Brazil:* **trem**) **rápido/correio para . . .**   From which platform does the express train/mail train leave for . . .

É directo ou tenho de mudar *(in Brazil: . . . . **de trocar)?*** Is it direct or do I have to change?

vagão-restaurante   dining-car

vagão-cama *(in Brazil:* **vagão-dormitório)**   sleeping car

sala de espera   waiting-room

carregador   porter

depósito de bagagens   left luggage office

O comboio vem à tabela *(in Brazil: . . . . **no horário certo)/ atrasado/adiantado?**   Will the train be on time/late/ early?

estação dos caminhos de ferro   railway station

de carro/by car

auto-estrada   motorway

estrada nacional   class A road

passagem de nível   level crossing

passagem de peões/passadeira   pedestrian crossing

sentido único   one way

perigo   danger

desvio   diversion

curva perigosa   dangerous bend

estacionamento proibido   no parking

trabalhos/obras *(in Brazil::* **trabalhadores)**   road works

estação de serviço   service station

bomba de gasolina   petrol pump

Mostre-me a sua carta de condução *(in Brazil:* **carteira de motorista/carta de direção).**   Show me your driving licence.

matrícula   registration number

avarias/car breakdown

Rebentou-me um pneu.   One of my tyres has burst.

A bateria está descarregada.   The battery is run down.

afinar os travões *(in Brazil:* **acertar os freios)** to adjust the brakes

Preciso de ar nos pneus.   I need air in the tyres.

uma lata de óleo   a tin of oil

água no radiador   water in the radiator

faróis   headlights

tubo de escape   exhaust pipe
velas   spark plugs
mudanças   gears
caixa de velocidades   gear-box
embraiagem   clutch
pára-brisas   windshield
limpa pára-brisas   wipers
guarda-lama   mud-guard
motor de arranque   starting motor
roda sobresselente   spare tyre
câmara de ar   inner tube
marcha atrás (in *Brazil:* **marcha a ré**)   reverse
ponto morto   neutral

acidentes/accidents

feridos/mortos   injured / dead
Mande chamar o médico.   Call for the doctor.
Desmaiou./Está a sangrar.   He has fainted./He is
   bleeding.
A ambulância já vem.   The ambulance is on its way.
Embateu em/Chocou com . . . It hit . . . It crashed against . .
camioneta   lorry, coach
carro de bois   oxen cart
bicicleta   bicycle
Tentava ultrapassar o outro.   He was trying to overtake
   the other.
Ia a grande velocidade.   He was going (travelling) at high
   speed.
Atropelou um cão.   He ran over a dog.
O carro derrapou.   The car skidded.
rua escorregadiça/escorregadia   slippery road
testemunhas   witnesses
Ouvi o barulho.   I heard the noise.

no consultório médico / at the doctor's

Estou constipado (*in Brazil:* **resfriado**).   I have a cold.
O senhor está com a gripe.   You (*m.*) have influenza.
receita/remédios   prescription / medicine (medicaments)

Tenho dores de cabeça/das costas/da garganta/da barriga.
  I have a head-ache/back-ache/sore throat/tummy-ache.
insolação sun-stroke
intoxicação alimentar food poisoning
enxaquec migraine
febre fever
Desloquei o braço/o tornozelo. I sprained my arm/my
  ankle.
Deite-se. Dispa-se. Vista-se. Lie down. Get undressed.
  Get dressed.
injecções/xarope/comprimidos/pomada/tónico injections/
  cough mixture/tablets/ointment/tonic
dar baixa ao hospital to go into hospital
Teve alta do hospital. He was discharged from hospital.
Estimo as melhoras. I hope you will get better (soon).
enfermeira/enfermeira-chefe nurse/sister
prisão de ventre constipation
tonturas dizzy spells
arrepios de frio cold shivers
fraco, fraca weak

dentista/dentist

dores de dentes toothache
Abra a boca. Open your mouth.
Vou tirar uma radiografia. I am going to take an X-ray.
Precisa de arrancar este dente. You need to have this
  tooth (pulled) out.
Este dente precisa de ser chumbado. This tooth needs to
  be filled.
Tem uma cárie. You have a decayed tooth.
Quanto é a consulta? How much is the consultation fee?
Está a doer-me/magoar-me. You are hurting me.

no hotel/at the hotel

A que horas é o pequeno-almoço (*in Brazil:* **café da
  manhã**)? What time is breakfast (served)?
Pode acordar-me às sete horas? Can you wake me up at
  seven?

O horário das refeições está no seu quarto. The list of meal times is in your room.

pensão completa/meia-pensão full board/half-board

só dormida room only

quarto de casal com casa de banho (*in Brazil:* **com banheiro**) double room with bathroom

quarto para pessoa só com chuveiro single room with shower

Preciso de uma outra almofada/cobertor. I need another pillow/blanket.

Como se acende/apaga a televisão/a luz? How do you switch on/off the T.V./the light?

Onde se pode alugar um automóvel? Where can one hire a car?

O ar condicionado/aquecimento central está avariado. The air conditioning/central heating is not working.

Como se abrem os estores? How do you work these blinds?

Estão incluidos o serviço e o imposto? Does that include all service and taxes?

Onde fica a piscina? Where is the swimming-pool?

Tenho uma reclamação/queixa a fazer I have a complaint to make.

Onde está o gerente? Where is the manager?

Gostei da estadia. I enjoyed my stay.

É muito amável. You are very kind.

Obrigado/Obrigada pela sua ajuda. Thank you for your help.

no restaurante/in the restaurant

Traga-me a ementa/a conta. Please bring me the menu/the bill.

garrafa de vinho tinto/branco bottle of red/white wine

pão com manteiga/compota bread and butter/jam

torrada toast

O que me recomenda/aconselha? What do you recommend?

prato do dia plate of the day

mal passado/bem passado/picante rare/well-done/spicy

Preciso de sal/pimenta/mustarda. I need salt/pepper/ mustard.

Não tenho guardanapo. I haven't a napkin.

Esqueceu-se da salada. You have forgotten the salad.

jarro de água jug of water

Não como carne/peixe. I don't eat meat/fish.

Este copo esta sujo. This glass is dirty.

Falta uma faça/uma colher/um garfo. A knife/spoon/fork is missing.

A refeição estava óptima/excelente. The meal was super/ excellent.

a gorjeta the tip

Fique com o troco. Keep the change.

Não quero mais. Basta./Chega. I don't want any more. Enough!

um pouco mais a little more

casas e situações domésticas/house and household (domestic situations)

anúncio advertisement

venda/compra/renda sale/purchase/rent

senhorio/inquilino/notário landlord/tenant/solicitor

escritura/câmara deeds/town hall

contribuição predial municipality rates

casas assoalhadas/divisões rooms (*not counting kitchen, bathroom*)

Já dei o sinal. I have already given the deposit.

Ela vai mudar-se. She is going to move (house).

orçamento/despesas estimate (budget)/expenses

O autoclismo não funciona. The flush is not working.

A torneira da banheira/do lavatório está a pingar. The tap of the bath/wash-basin is dripping.

Os canos estão entupidos. The pipes are blocked.

A mulher a dias hoje fez gazeta. Today the daily has not turned up.

passar a ferro/engomar to iron

lavar a louça/a roupa to wash up/wash clothes

Esta saia precisa de ser limpa a seco. This skirt needs to be dry-cleaned.

Tem muitas nódoas. It has many stains.

O frigorífico está sujo.   The refrigerator is dirty.

Esta mesa deve ser encerada.   This table should be polished.

A campaínha da porta não toca.   The door bell is not ringing.

quarto/sala de visitas/cozinha   bedroom/sitting-room/kitchen

casa de jantar/casa de banho/varanda   dining-room/bathroom/balcony

O leite está azedo.   The milk has gone sour.

As maçãs estão pôdres.   The apples are rotten.

Há falta de batatas.   There is a shortage of potatoes.

Quero que me descasques estas cebolas.   I want you to peel these onions for me.

Vou descascar estas laranjas.   I am going to peel these oranges.

Os padeiros estão em greve.   The bakers are on strike.

Havia uma grande bicha *(in Brazil:* **fila) no talho** *(in Brazil:* **açougue.)**   There was a long queue at the butcher's.

compras em geral/shopping (in general)

drogaria   drugstore

mercearia   grocer

tabacaria   tobacconist

Quero dois maços de cigarros ingleses.   I want two packets of English cigarettes.

De que marca?   Which brand?

Quanto custa?   How much is it?

caixa/carteira de fósforos   box/book of matches

postais ilustrados/revista/jornal   postcards/magazine/newspaper

rolo a cores *(in Brazil:* **filme em cores)**   colour film

rolo a preto e branco *(in Brazil:* **filme em . . .)**   black and white film

Onde se pode mandar revelar?   Where can one have it developed?

Onde fica a esquadra/o posto de polícia?   Where is the police station?

estação dos correios/selos/via aérea   post-office/stamps/by air mail

impressos para telegramas/vale postal forms for
telegrams/postal money order
Onde se levantam as encomendas postais? Where does
one collect registered parcels?
sapataria shoe-shop
Estes sapatos não me servem. These shoes do not fit me.
Qual é o tamanho/o número que calça/que veste? What
size/number do you take in shoes/clothes?
salto alto/salto baixo/salto raso high heel/low heel/flat
heel
secção de retrosaria/de chapelaria department of
haberdashery/millinery
tecidos/fazenda/seda *(in Brazil.* **sêda)/algodão/la**
materials/woollen cloth/silk/cotton/wool
Este casaco *(in Brazil:* **paletó) está-me apertado.** This coat
is tight on me.
Esta cor *(in Brazil:* **côr) não me fica bem.** This colour does
not suit me.

roupa or vestuário e cores / clothes and colours

fato *(in Brazil:* **terno)/saia/casaco** suit/skirt/coat (jacket)
vestido/calças/calções *(in Brazil:* **calças de esporte)** dress/
trousers/shorts
fato de banho *(in Brazil:* **maiô de banho)** swimsuit
sobretudo/camisola/blusa/lenço overcoat/jumper/
blouse/handkerchief
impermeável/guarda-chuva/cinto/luvas raincoat/
umbrella/belt/gloves
cinta/meias/cuecas/soutien girdle/stockings/pants/bra
peúgas/camisa de noite *(in Brazil:* **camisola)/roupa de
interior** socks/nightdress/underclothes
gravata/pijama/colete/camisa tie/pyjamas/waistcoat/
shirt
verde/azul/branco/preto/roxo green/blue/white/black/
purple
encarnado/vermelho/amarelo red/dark red/yellow
cinzento/castanho *(in Brazil:* **marron)/côr-de-rosa** grey/
brown/pink
côr-de-laranja/claro/escuro/dourado orange/light/dark/
gold

prateado/beige/côr de camelo/creme silver/beige/camel colour/cream

cabeleireiro, barbeiro/hairdresser, barber

Quero uma mise/permanente/pintura *(in Brazil:* **tintura)** I want a set/perm/tint
um penteado simples/elegante a simple/elegant hairstyle
um corte/só aparado/ripado *(in Brazil:* **desfiado/a unhas feitas)** a cut/only trimmed/back-combed
Deixe-o comprido/curto. Leave it long/short.
Tenho o cabelo encaracolado/ondulado/liso. I have curly/wavy/straight hair.
Não quero o cabelo frisado. I don't want my hair frizzy.
Quanto tempo preciso de ficar debaixo do secador? How long do I need to be under the dryer?
Quero as minhas unhas arranjadas. I want my nails done.
Quero só fazer a barba. I just want a shave.
Não toque no bigode ou nas suiças/patilhas. Don't touch the moustache or side-whiskers/sideburns.
Faça o risco ao lado/ao meio. Part it on the side/centre.

divertimentos/entertainment and pastimes

corrida de cavalos/de bicicleta horse race/bicycle race
tourada/toureiro/espada/perícia bullfight/bullfighter/sword/skill
desafio de futebol *(in Brazil:* **jogo de futebol)/empate** football match/draw
jogar as cartas/o xadrez/apostar to play cards/chess/to bet
bilheteira//lotação esgotada *(in Brazil:* **bilheteria/ingressos esgotados)** ticket office/house sold out
barco à vela/à motor/remar sailing boat/motor boat/to row
corte de ténis *(in Brazil:* **quadra de ténis)** tennis court
campo de golfe golf course

Appendix: Verbs

Regular, radical-changing. irregular, and verbs requiring a preposition

Revision table of regular verbs

(only the endings are given)
Indicative mood

PRESENT TENSE			PAST DEFINITE			IMPERFECT		
-ar	**-er**	**-ir**	**-ar**	**-er**	**-ir**	**-ar**	**-er**	**-ir**
-o	-o	-o	-ei	-i	-i	-ava	-ia	-ia
-as	-es	-es	-aste	-este	-iste	-avas	-ias	-ias
-a	-e	-e	-ou	-eu	-iu	-ava	-ia	-ia
-amos	-emos	-imos	-ámos	-emos	-imos	-ávamos	-íamos	-íamos
-am	-em	-em	-aram	-eram	-iram	-avam	-iam	-iam

FUTURE*			CONDITIONAL*			*Past participle*		
-ar	**-er**	**-ir**	**-ar**	**-er**	**-ir**	**-ar**	**-er**	**-ir**
-ei	-ei	-ei	-ia	-ia	-ia	-ado	-ido	-ido
-ás	-ás	-ás	-ias	-ias	-ias	*(used in forming*		
-á	-á	-á	-ia	-ia	-ia	*compound tenses, such*		
-emos	-emos	-emos	-íamos	-íamos	-íamos	*as the perfect, pluperfect*		
-ão	-ão	-ão	-iam	-iam	-iam	*and others)*		

Subjunctive mood

PRESENT			IMPERFECT			FUTURE**		
-ar	**-er**	**-ir**	**-ar**	**-er**	**-ir**	**-ar**	**-er**	**-ir**
-e	-a	-a	-asse	-esse	-isse	-ar	-er	-ir
-es	-as	-as	-asses	-esses	-isses	-ares	-eres	-ires
-e	-a	-a	-asse	-esse	-isse	-ar	-er	-ir
-emos	-amos	-amos	-ássemos	-êssemos	-íssemos	-armos	-ermos	-irmos
-em	-am	-am	-assem	-essem	-issem	-arem	-erem	-irem

Imperative				*Present participle*		
-ar	**-er**	**-ir**		**-ar**	**-er**	**-ir**
-a	-e	-e	(you, *familiar*)	-ando	-endo	-indo
-e	-a	-a	(you, *formal*)			
-emos	-amos	-amos	(let us . . .)			
-ai	-ei	-i	(you, *plural, classical language*)			
-em	-am	-am	(you *plural*)			

NOTES:

* When forming the future and conditional of the indicative mood, the endings given above are added to the infinitive, without removing its ending: e. g. fal|ar|ei, fal|ar|ia. In the other tenses, the infinitive endings (-ar, -er, -ir) are dropped: fal|o, fa|ei, etc.

** The personal infinitive of these regular verbs is formed in the same way as the future of the subjunctive, given above.

Radical-changing verbs

The stem of the infinitive changes only in the 1st person singular of the present tense indicative and consequently in all persons of the subjunctive.

e to **i**

INFINITIVE	PRESENT TENSE	PRESENT SUBJUNCTIVE
seguir (to follow)	**sigo**	**siga, -as, -a, -amos, -am**
preferir (to prefer)	**prefiro**	**prefira** etc
mentir (to lie)	**minto**	**minta** etc
vestir (to dress)	**visto**	**vista** etc
servir (to serve)	**sirvo**	**sirva** etc
sentir (to feel)	**sinto**	**sinta** etc
divertir-se (to enjoy)	**divirto-me**	**me divirta** etc
despir (to undress)	**dispo**	**dispa** etc
conseguir (to succeed, manage, achieve)	**consigo**	**consiga** etc
repetir (to repeat)	**repito**	**repita** etc

o to **u**

cobrir (to cover)	**cubro**	**cubra** etc
descobrir (to discover)	**descubro**	**descubra** etc
dormir (to sleep)	**durmo**	**durma** etc
tossir (to cough)	**tusso**	**tussa** etc

But verbs **subir** (to climb, to go up), **fugir** (to run away, to flee), **destruir** (to destroy) and **construir** (to build) have the following changes in the present indicative, e.g.:

eu subo   **nós subimos**
tu sobes   **sobem**
ele sobe

Other radical-changing verbs, which alter in the 1st person singular and subjunctive only:

perder (to lose)	**perco**	**perca** etc
medir (to measure)	**meço**	**meça** etc
valer (to be worth)	**valho**	**valha** etc
pedir (to ask for)	**peço**	**peça** etc
ouvir (to hear, listen)	**ouço**	**ouça** etc

Spelling-change verbs

The term 'orthographical-changing' is used to describe verbs in which the last consonant of the stem is modified or changed in certain persons and tenses in order to preserve the sound of the infinitive. The most common examples are as follows:

-**car**→**qu** before **e** or **i**
brin**c**ar (to play)→brin**qu**ei (I played)

-**çar**→**c** before **e** or **i**
come**ç**ar (to begin)→come**c**ei (I began)

-cer→**ç** before **a**, **o** or **u**
conhecer (to know)→conheço (I know)

-gar→**gu** before **e** or **i**
chegar (to arrive)→chegue (I arrived)

-ger, -gir→**j** before **a**, **o** or **u**
fugir (to flee)→fujo (I flee)

-guer, -guir→**g** before **a**, **o** or **u**
perseguir (to pursue)→persigo (I pursue)

Table of irregular verbs

In order to make it easier for the student to learn these verbs, we are giving them in order of similarity, where applicable. Only the 1st person singular is given in those tenses (imperfect, future etc) where the *endings* are the same as for the regular tenses.

dar	**estar**	**ser**	**ir**
(to give)	*(to be)*	*(to be)*	*(to go)*
PRESENT TENSE			
dou	estou	sou	vou
dás	estás	és	vais
dá	está	é	vai
damos	estamos	somos	vamos
dão	estão	são	vão
PAST DEFINITE			
dei	estive	fui	fui
deste	estiveste	foste	foste
deu	esteve	foi	foi
demos	estivemos	fomos	fomos
deram	estiveram	foram	foram

IMPERFECT

dava	estava	era	ia

FUTURE

darei	estarei	serei	irei

CONDITIONAL

daria	estaria	seria	iria

PRESENT SUBJUNCTIVE

dê	esteja	seja	vá
dês	estejas	sejas	vás
dê	esteja	seja	vá
dêmos	estejamos	sejamos	vamos
dêem	estejam	sejam	vão

IMPERFECT SUBJUNCTIVE

desse	estivesse	fosse	fosse

FUTURE SUBJUNCTIVE

der	estiver	for	for

PERSONAL INFINITIVE

dar	estar	ser	ir
dares	estares	seres	ires
dar	estar	ser	ir
darmos	estarmos	sermos	irmos
darem	estarem	serem	irem

IMPERATIVE

dá	está	sê	vai
dê	esteja	seja	vá
dêmos	estejamos	sejamos	vamos
(dai)	(estai)	(sede)	(ide)
dêem	estejam	sejam	vão

PAST PARTICIPLE

dado	estado	sido	ido

PRESENT PARTICIPLE

dando	estando	sendo	indo

| **ter** | **vir** | **ver** | **pôr** |
| *(to have)* | *(to come)* | *(to see)* | *(to put)* |

PRESENT TENSE

tenho	venho	vejo	ponho
tens	vens	vês	pões
tem	vem	vê	põe
temos	vimos	vemos	pomos
têm	vêm	vêem	põem

PAST DEFINITE

tive	vim	vi	pus
tiveste	vieste	viste	puseste
teve	veio	viu	pôs
tivemos	viemos	vimos	pusemos
tiveram	vieram	viram	puseram

IMPERFECT

tinha	vinha	via	punha

FUTURE

terei	virei	verei	porei

CONDTTIONAL

teria	viria	veria	poria

PRESENT SUBJUNCTIVE

tenha	venha	veja	ponha

IMPERFECT SUBJUNCTIVE

tivesse	viesse	visse	pusesse

FUTURE SUBJUNCTIVE

tiver	vier	vir	puser

PERSONAL INFINITIVE

ter	vir	ver	pôr

IMPERATIVE

tem	vem	vê	põe
tenha	venha	veja	ponha

tenhamos	venhamos	vejamos	ponhamos
tende	vinde	(vede)	(ponde)
tenham	venham	vejam	ponham

PAST PARTICIPLE

tido	vindo	visto	posto

PRESENT PARTICIPLE

tendo	vindo	vendo	pondo

trazer	dizer	fazer	saber	haver	poder
(to bring)	*(to say)*	*(to do, make)*	*(to know)*	*(to have)*	*(to be able to)*

PRESENT TENSE

trago	digo	faço	sei	hei	posso
trazes	dizes	fazes	sabes	hás	podes
traz	diz	faz	sabe	há	pode
trazemos	dizemos	fazemos	sabemos	havemos	podemos
trazem	dizem	fazem	sabem	hão	podem

PAST DEFINITE

trouxe	disse	fiz	soube	houve	pude
trouxeste	disseste	fizeste	soubeste	houveste	pudeste
trouxe	disse	fez	soube	houve	pôde
trouxemos	dissemos	fizemos	soubemos	houvemos	pudemos
trouxeram	disseram	fizeram	souberam	houveram	puderam

IMPERFECT

trazia	dizia	fazia	sabia	havia	podia

FUTURE

trarei	direi	farei	*(regular)*	*(regular)*	*(regular)*
trarás	dirás	farás			
trará	dirá	fará			
traremos	diremos	faremos			
trarão	dirão	farão			

CONDITIONAL

traria	diria	faria	*(regular)*	*(regular)*	*(regular)*
trarias	dirias	farias			
traria	diria	faria			
traríamos	diríamos	faríamos			
trariam	diriam	fariam			

PRESENT SUBJUNCTIVE

traga	diga	faça	saiba	haja	possa
tragas	digas	faças	saibas	hajas	possas
traga	diga	faça	saiba	haja	possa
tragamos	digamos	façamos	saibamos	hajamos	possamos
tragam	digam	façam	saibam	hajam	possam

IMPERFECT SUBJUNCTIVE

trouxesse	dissesse	fizesse	soubesse	houvesse	pudesse

FUTURE SUBJUNCTIVE

trouxer	disser	fizer	souber	houver	puder

PERSONAL INFINITIVE

trazer	dizer	fazer	saber	haver	poder

PAST PARTICIPLE

trazido	dito	feito	sabido	havido	podido

PRESENT PARTICIPLE

trazendo	dizendo	fazendo	sabendo	havendo	podendo

IMPERATIVE

traz (e)	diz (e)	faz (e)	sabe	há	pode
traga	diga	faça	saiba	haja	possa
tragamos	digamos	façamos	saibamos	hajamos	possamos
(trazei)	(dizei)	(fazei)	(sabei)	(havei)	(podei)
tragam	digam	façam	saibam	hajam	possam

ler	**crer**	**querer**	**rir***	**caber**
(to read)	*(to think, believe)*	*(to want)*	*(to laugh)*	*(to fit in, be contained)*

PRESENT TENSE

leio	creio	quero	rio	caibo
lês	crês	queres	ris	*(otherwise*
lê	crê	quer(e)	ri	*conjugated*
lemos	cremos	queremos	rimos	*like* saber *in*
lêem	crêem	querem	riem	*all tenses)*

PAST DEFINITE

li	cri	quis	ri
leste	creste	quiseste	riste
leu	creu	quis	riu
lemos	cremos	quisemos	rimos
leram	creram	quiseram	riram

IMPERFECT

lia	cria	queria	ria

FUTURE

lerei	crerei	quererei	rirei

CONDITIONAL

leria	creria	quereria	riria

PRESENT SUBJUNCTIVE

leia	creia	queira	ria

IMPERFECT SUBJUNCTIVE

lesse	cresse	quisesse	risse

FUTURE SUBJUNCTIVE

ler	crer	quiser	rir

PERSONAL INFINITIVE

ler	crer	querer	rir

PAST PARTICIPLE

lido	crido	querido	rido

PRESENT PARTICIPLE

lendo	crendo	querendo	rindo

IMPERATIVE

lê	crê	quer(e)	ri
leia	creia	queira	ria
leiamos	creiamos	queiramos	riamos
(lede)	crede	querei	ride
leiam	creiam	queiram	riam

* **Sorrir** to smile, is conjugated like **rir**.

Some remarks

1 The SIMPLE PLUPERFECT may be encountered in writing but is seldom used in speech, when the compound pluperfect **(tinha falado)** is preferred. In regular verbs you add **ra** to the stem of the infinitive: e.g. **falara, comera, partira**.

In irregular verbs the termination you add to the stem of the past definite is the same as for the imperfect and future of the subjunctive mood: e.g. **dissera, fizera, fora, dera, trouxera, vira, tivera.**

2 The subjunctive mood also has its own compound tenses: the perfect, **tenha falado**, the pluperfect, **tivesse falado**, and the compound future, **tiver falado.**

3 Haver is an auxiliary verb which sometimes replaces the verb **ter** in compound tenses, especially in literary works. It is then fully conjugated as shown above.

Haver as an *impersonal verb* only uses the 3rd person singular in all tenses. i.e. **há**, which means 'there is'/'there are' etc.

Some verbs which require a preposition before the infinitive of another verb

acabar de to finish (doing something)	Acabo de comer. i.e. 'I have just (finished) eaten'.
aconselhar a to advise	Aconselho-o a ver o médico.
ajudar a to help	Ela ajuda-me a lavar a louça.
acabar por to end up (doing . . .)	Ele acabou por consentir.
começar a to begin	Ele começou a falar.
começar por to begin by . . .	Ele começou por dizer.
esquecer-se de to forget	Esqueci-me de te dizer que . . .
lembrar-se de to remember	Não me lembro do seu nome.
gostar de to like	Gosto de comer. *(preposition also needed before a noun)*
obrigar a to force, compel	Obriguei-a a dizer a verdade.
precisar de to need	Preciso de falar com ele. *(also needed before a noun)*
voltar a (to do it) again	Voltei a vê-lo.
voltar para to return to (do something)	Voltei para te ver.
pensar em to think of	Pensei em falar contigo.
pedir para to ask (to)	Pedi-lhe para fazer isso.

Some verbs followed by a preposition

assistir a to attend	Assisti a uma tourada.
aproximar-se de to go near	Aproximei-me dele.
casar-se com to get married	Ela casou-se com um inglês.
chegar a to arrive at	Cheguei à conclusão.
	Cheguei a Faro.
dar com to come across, to bump into	Dei com a Manuela no armazém.
dar por to notice	Não dei por ela.

dar para to overlook	O meu quarto dá para o jardim.
dar para to be enough for	Esta carne dá para cinco pessoas.
acreditar em to believe	Acredito em ti.
duvidar de to doubt	Duvido da sua palavra.
encontrar-se com to meet (by arrangement. mostly)	Vou-me encontrar com eles.
ir a, ir para to go to	Vou a Paris em negócios. **(ir a** *implies a shorter stay than* **ir para)**
olhar para to look at	Ele olhou para mim.
parecer-se com to look like, resemble	Ela parece-se com o pai.
pegar em to pick up	Ele pegou na mala.
(*In Brazil:* **pegar** *without preposition*)	
queixar-se de to complain about	Eu queixei-me da comida.
reparar em to notice	Reparei no teu vestido.
sonhar com to dream of	Sonhei contigo.
sorrir para to smile at	Ela sorriu para a menina.
vir a, vir para to come	Ele veio a Londres. **(vir a** *implies a shorter stay than* **vir para)**

Key to Exercises

CHAPTER 1

Exercise 1: 1 A rapariga. 2 O rapaz. 3 O escritório. 4 A casa. 5 As flores. 6 Os empregos. 7 Os gatos. 8 As alunas. 9 A mesa. 10 As mesas.

Exercise 2: 1 Uma viagem. 2 Um escritório. 3 Um avião. 4 Uma cidade. 5 Um bilhete. 6 Uns homens. 7 Umas mulheres. 8 Umas viagens. 9 Uns escritórios. 10 Umas raparigas.

Exercise 3: 1 I have. 2 Have you (Do you have)? 3 We don't have. 4 You have *(pl)*. 5 Has she? 6 You do not have *(pl formal)*. 7 Haven't they? 8 (Eu) Não tenho dinheiro. 9 A senhora tem um bilhete? 10 Eles têm bons empregos. 11 Vocês têm uma casa? 12 Tu tens um escritório. 13 (Nós) Temos fome. 14 Não há uma mesa. 15 Há quanto tempo fala inglês?

Exercise P. 1 1 Não. A senhora Smith é inglesa. 2 Ela agora mora em Lisboa. 3 Sim, tem. 4 Não, como auditora de uma grande companhia. 5 Ela tem um escritório no Estoril. 6 O marido dela é professor de inglês. 7 Não. A Maria Helena é do Algarve. 8 Ela é médica. 9 Não. Lisboa é a capital de Portugal. 10 Sim, Londres é uma cidade linda. 11 Não, não falo português. 12 *(alt. A)* Sim, sou professora. *(alt. B)* Não não sou.

CHAPTER 2

Exercise 4: 1 Sou inglesa. 2 O senhor é o gerente deste hotel? 3 Ele é aborrecido. 4 Ela é uma secretária. 5 Isto é muito importante. 6 Nós somos amigas. 7 Eles são velhos. 8 São estas as malas? 9 These suitcases are not mine. 10 This is impossible. 11 I am not a secretary, I am a teacher. 12 We are friends. 13 Are you *(pl informal)* married?

Exercise 5: 1 Estou em Londres. 2 Tu estás cansada? 3 Ela não está em casa. 4 Estamos a trabalhar todos os dias. 5 Eles estão enganados. 6 O combóio *(in Brazil:* trem) está atrasado. 7 I am eating. 8 Are you at home today? 9 We are not mistaken. 10 You *(sing. formal)* are hungry. 11 They are looking beautiful. 12 The girls are ready.

Exercise 6: 1 O livro está na mesa. 2 A mulher esta à porta. 3 Ela vai pelo parque. 4 O escritório do tio Tomás. 5 Estou ao telefone. 6 A água está no copo. 7 Estou aqui em férias. 8 We are going to the market. 9 I am going home. 10 She is in the bathroom. 11 In a situation like this (one). 12 He came in through the window. 13 I am speaking of the accident. 14 He gave the money to the boy.

CHAPTER 3

Exercise 7: 1 We are looking for a house. 2 They don't speak Portuguese very well, but they understand everything. 3 She never accepts my invitation. 4 What (will) you take? 5 She opens the window. (She is opening the window.) 6 I study every day. 7 You *(pl informal)* don't eat much. 8 I am leaving at 9 o'clock. 9 You work very much (a lot). 10 Do you buy (are you buying) the tickets?

Exercise 8: 1 Meu irmão procura um emprego em Moçambique. 2 Ele aprende português. 3 Precisa de ajuda? 4 Aceito o seu convite com prazer. 5 Bebem e fumam demasiado. 6 O comboio parte à tabela. *(in Brazil:* O trem parte no horário certo.) 7 Ele vende o carro. 8 Hoje não compro nada. 9 Minha irmã não come à uma hora. 10 Ela está de dieta.

Exercise P. 3: dizia-me; há; perto; dois minutos daqui; por aqui; a direito; passar; vê logo; ir ao; fica; um pouco; melhor; apanhar; está ali; esquerda; virar; esquina; sabem; está; Claro; conhecem; a palma da mão.

Exercise 9: 1 Which is the nearest station from here? 2 What is your address? 3 She never does what I want. 4 Why don't you go by car? 5 I believe it is very far. 6 How is business going? 7 I do not know whom I should pay. 8 Onde vai? 9 Quanto devo? 10 Não me disse o seu nome. 11 Que disse

você? 12 Quem é aquele homen lindo? 13 Quando vai a
França? 14 As chaves que ela me deu não são minhas.

Exercise 10: 1 That shop on the corner. 2 We are going to
that beach. 3 What is this? 4 This is a computer. 5 Please shut
that door. 6 This is my husband and that is my son. 7 These
keys are not mine. 8 Esta casa é grande. 9 O que é isso?
10 Não quero aqueles livros. 11 Isto é impossível. 12 Ele está
naquele hotel. 13 Esta mala é daquele homen. 14 Os bilhetes
estão nesta mala de senhora.

CHAPTER 4

Exercise 11: 1 I like your home/house very much. 2 This is
your glass and that one (over there) is his. 3 Your daughter is
very nice/charming. 4 Our holidays begin in June. 5 My wife
always arrives late. 6 São estas as suas malas? 7 O meu
telefone está sempre avariado. 8 Isto não é meu. 9 Não sei o
nome deles. 10 A vossa casa é muito longe. 11 A nossa filha
chega amanhã. 12 O amigo dele é americano.

Exercise 12: 1 I finish work/(working) at six o'clock. 2 We
are going to spend a fortnight on the beach. 3 She has four
brothers (*also meaning* brothers and sisters). 4 The book costs
1200 escudos. 5 This lift only takes five people. 6 I go to Paris
every four weeks. 7 My birthday is on the 20th September.
8 Ele começa o trabalho às oito horas. 9 Ela tem dois rapazes e
três raparigas. 10 Eu escrevo à minha mãe de cinco em cinco
dias. 11 Ele parte a vinte de maio (*or* Ele parte no dia vinte de
maio). 12 Ele não trabalha há dez dias. 13 Tenho trinta e cinco
anos. 14 São seis menos um quarto.

Exercise 13: 1 Next week I am going (I go) to my aunt's
(house). 2 Last month my brother went to work in Brazil.
3 My children (sons) will arrive in a fortnight (in 15 days'
time). 4 Tonight we are going to the theatre. 5 Spring is my
favourite season. 6 Yesterday it was very cold. 7 The day after
tomorrow we shall have the results of our examinations.
8 Vou passar o Natal com os meus amigos em Lisboa. 9 Este
ano não tenho férias. 10 Ela vai passar o verão no Algarve.
11 Ontem esteve (fez) calor. 12 Faço anos no domingo.
13 Amanhã de manhã começo o trabalho (começo a trabalhar).
14 Julho, agosto e setembro são meses muito quentes em
Portugal.

CHAPTER 5

Exercise 14: 1 Hoje o tempo está mau. 2 Ela é uma boa secretária. 3 Não sei onde está o meu mapa francês. 4 Minha irmã é mais velha do que eu. 5 A minha amiga é espanhola, mas o marido dela é inglês. 6 É uma boa coisa que você faz. 7 Há muitas pessoas simpáticas neste mundo (*or* Há muita gente simpática neste mundo). 8 O meu colega está muito contente no Brasil. 9 O Mercado Comum é uma comunidade europeia. 10 A mãe da minha amiga e (uma) poetisa. 11 Tenho um grande carro verde. 12 Meu primo é um bom escritor e a mulher dele é também uma boa escritora. 13 O António é um jornalista português. 14 Esta galinha está crua.

Exercise 15: 1 Duas salas. 2 Meus irmãos. 3 As flores são lindas. 4 Estes problemas são difíceis. 5 No verão há muita gente nas praias. 6 Três estudantes ingleses. 7 Quatro lençóis. 8 Os meus amigos são muito amáveis. 9 Não conheço estes homens. 10 As crianças alemãs não gostam de cães. 11 Compro cinco pães todos os dias. 12 Ela gosta de todos os animais. 13 A minha irmã tem olhos azuis. 14 Tenho as mãos sujas. 15 Estes limões são bons. 16 Meus pais estão sempre tão felizes / contentes.

Exercise 16: 1 Yesterday I received a letter from my friend. 2 We liked your home very much. 3 Last week we visited a very modern school. 4 They have left for Brazil. 5 Have you sold your house yet (already)? 6 No, we haven't sold our house yet. 7 They haven't written yet. 8 Não compreendi. 9 O que beberam eles? 10 Já comi. 11 Quando partiram eles? 12 A que horas partiu o comboio? 13 Não abrimos a janela. 14 Ele não comeu ontem à noite. 15 Você falou com a sua mãe? 16 Conheci o seu irmão em Lisboa.

Exercise 17: 1 Come here. 2 Speak slowly. 3 Don't make a noise. 4 Go that way. 5 Don't be silly. 6 Be still. 7 Bring the wine list. 8 Fale devagar. 9 Abramos a janela. 10 Fechem a porta. 11 Não comam tão depressa. 12 Vejamos . . . . 13 Venham já. 14 Vamos! 15 Não falem tão alto. 16 Não diga nada.

CHAPTER 6

Exercise 18: 1 When I was a child I learnt everything more easily. (. . . it was easier to learn.) 2 I used to eat a lot, (Before, I ate a lot,) but not now. 3 We used to go to the beach every day. 4 Yesterday we went to the country. 5 It was underneath this tree that I used to sit. 6 What were you doing? 7 I was taking a bath. 8 A que horas tomou o seu pequeno-almoço? 9 Dizia-me por favor onde é (fica) a paragem do autocarro (in *Brazil.* a parada do ônibus?) 10 Soube que o seu irmão ía para a Africa, é verdade? 11 Chovia a cântaros quando saímos. 12 Ele ouvia enquanto eu falava. 13 Já comia. 14 Ontem (à noite) jantei com a minha sogra.

Exercise 18a: 1 The plane took six hours to arrive there. 2 Today, I do not want to play with the children; I prefer to play chess. 3 He comes here many times. 4 She went to New York and from there she went to Mexico. 5 Doctor, how many tablets do I have to take? 6 I had to take out (draw) money from my deposit account. 7 Como está o tempo aí? 8 As suas luvas estão aí. 9 A paragem do autocarro (*in Brazil:* A parada do ônibus) fica (está) ali. 10 Cá estou (Aqui estou). 11 Vejo um barco acolá. 12 As suas chaves estão aqui.

Exercise 19: 1 Give him/her my regards. 2 She rang me up last night. 3 She/he saw him last week. 4 I don't know them well. 5 They visit us every year. 6 We want to see him. 7 I am going to help you/her. 8 You *(pl)* help him very much. 9 He does not want the apples but I am going to give them to him. 10 You live near me. 11 I don't eat (I shan't eat, I am not eating) without you. 12 Come with me now to have a coffee and then (afterwards) I'll come with you to the hairdresser. 13 The dogs are with us, but the cats are with them *(f)*. 14 Who told you that? (Who told it to you?)

Exercise 20: 1 Mostre-nos o que encontrou (achou). 2 Vá procurá-la. (*in Brazil:* Vá buscar a ela.) 3 Estas flores são para mim? 4 Antes que me esqueça tenho de lhes dizer . . . 5 Ele esperou por nós. 6 Venha comigo. 7 Não há segredos entre nós. 8 Conto contigo. 9 Ele não mo emprestou. 10 Eles ajudam-no. 11 Minha mãe não me telefonou. 12 Não preciso dele. 13 Chamei-o mas ele não me ouviu. 14 Vi-os a semana passada. 15 Ele vai vê-la.

CHAPTER 7

Exercise 21: 1 Do you want (to take/to have) tea or coffee?
2 I want neither tea nor coffee - I prefer an orange juice.
3 I either go to the cinema or stay at home watching television,
I am not sure yet. 4 I have never seen an exhibition so well
organized. 5 He has no scruples at all. 6 I shall never again
buy electrical items (appliances) second hand. 7 You have
nothing to do with it. (*also* It is none of your business.)
8 No-one speaks English here. 9 I don't know anything.
10 We did not go anywhere.

Exercise 22: 1 Alguém aqui fala inglês? 2 O senhor pediu-me
uma colher ou uma faca? 3 Nem uma nem outra, pedi-lhe um
garfo. 4 Ele tem algumas esperanças. 5 Cada qual tem o seu
gosto. 6 Está tudo caríssimo. 7 Tem quaisquer revistas
inglesas? 8 São ambos escritores. 9 O jantar estava péssimo.
10 A minha tia está muito mal. 11 Ele é o homem mais rico do
mundo. 12 Tenho boas notícias para si. 13 Ela está tão feliz
como eu. 14 Camões foi o maior poeta português.

Exercise 23: 1 Quando lhe escreverá? (*also* Quando lhe vai
escrever?) 2 Ele tem de trabalhar muito. 3 Não o tomaremos.
4 Começarei a minha história. 5 Quem ganhará?
6 Chegar-emos no próximo mês. 7 Seria a verdade? 8 I should
say he is lying. 9 I shall not forget you. 10 I would do
everything for her. 11 They will give him/her/you my new
address. 12 I will go to Japan. 13 I have to go to the dentist.
14 Will it be very expensive?

CHAPTER 8

Exercise 24: 1 She had already studied Portuguese when she
was a child. 2 This year there have been many plane
accidents. 3 The woman was already dead when the doctor
arrived. 4 The tables were already laid but the guests had not
arrived yet. 5 I had never seen so many people in my life.
6 She was expelled from the school. 7 It is said (They say) that
the firm (Messrs) Agiota & Co. is going bankrupt. 8 One must
not deceive (cheat, mislead) others. 9 They had not washed
themselves yet. (They had not had a wash.) 10 The weather
has been bad.

Exercise 25: 1 They felt (were) disappointed. 2 I got up very early. 3 He never remembers my birthday. 4 She got dressed in a hurry. 5 He smells awful because he never washes himself. (. . . he never has a wash.) 6 How do you say 'table' in Portuguese? 7 They looked at each other. 8 Help yourself while the food is hot. 9 We don't know each other. 10 I complained to the police. 11 Go away. 12 It is sunny. 13 I forgot him. (about him.) 14 English newspapers are sold here.

Exercise 26: 1 Lembro-me dele. 2 Não me sentia bem. 3 Queixámo-nos da comida. 4 Tem chovido muito este ano. 5 Já tinha posto a carta no correio. 6 Bebe-se muito vinho em Portugal mas os portugueses nunca se embriagam. 7 A janela estava aberta. 8 A lotaria foi ganha por uma mulher pobre. 9 A minha saia estava rota. 10 Foram todos presos. 11 Eles olharam-se um ao outro. 12 Não tenho via jado este ano. 13 Ouve-se muita musica inglesa em Portugal. 14 Não quero servir-me. 15 Vimo-nos por acaso. 16 Aqui vendem-se jornais.

CHAPTER 9

Exercise 27: 1 It is necessary for them to study hard. (They must study hard.) 2 It is hoped they do not come in late. 3 Perhaps (Maybe) I will go out tomorrow. 4 I want you to do that at once. 5 Tell him not to come in until I call him. 6 I hope your wife is better. 7 I don't think he is a good football player. 8 We want a man who has the courage of his convictions. 9 Whether I like it or not I have to attend the meeting tomorrow. 10 Diga-lhe que não vá à reunião. 11 Embora eu não fale portugûes muito bem, compreendo tudo. 12 Quer que lhe traga a lista dos vinhos? 13 É melhor que eu vá agora. 14 Não creio que haja jornais hoje. 15 Eles têm pena (Lamentam) que não possa vir esta noite. 16 Por favor não faça nenhum barulho.

Exercise 28: 1 It was a pity (a shame) he could not come. 2 I wanted you *(pl)* to learn Portuguese as quickly as possible. 3 I did not see any house that pleased me. (. . . that I liked.) 4 Perhaps he had already left. 5 If it were not so expensive, we would buy a farm in the Algarve. 6 We did not want you *(pl)* to bring presents. 7 1 don't know whether it is raining. 8 If it rains I shall take an umbrella. 9 Until the factory workers go

back to (resume) work, we cannot increase production.
10 Come to our house whenever you want. 11 As soon as you
get a job in Mozambique, let me know (tell me). 12 Do what
you can. 13 Invite *(pl)* whom you wish. 14 He who (Whoever)
wants to come along with me, let him come.

Exercise 29: 1 Assim que puderes, telefona-me por favor.
2 Se ele não fosse tão preguiçoso (mandrião), não teria perdido
esse emprego. 3 Foi preciso que eles chamassem a polícia.
(also. Foi preciso chamarem a polícia.) 4 Disse-lhes para se
irem embora. *(also: Disse-lhes que se fossem embora.)* 5 Diga o
que disser, eu não acredito que ela seja desonesta. 6 Quando
me reformar escreverei muitos livros. 7 Faça como quiser.
(also: Faça o que quiser.) 8 Aconteça o que acontecer, e apesar
do tempo (clima) sempre amarei a Inglaterra. 9 Não havia
ninguém que falasse inglês. 10 Enquanto estiverem em minha
casa, são meus convidados. 11 Lamentei que não pudessem
vir. *(also: Lamentei não poderem vir.)* 12 Se você perdeu esta
oportunidade foi porque quis. 13 Embora protestassem *(or:*
Tivessem protestado) muitas vezes a situação continuou a ser a
mesma.

*Note: The alternatives given above demonstrate the use of the
personal infinitive explained in chapter 10.*

CHAPTER 10

Exercise 30: 1 This book is for us to read. 2 I don't want to
buy the car unless you agree (without your agreeing). 3 It is a
shame (a pity) you cannot come next Sunday. 4 It was good (a
good thing) that you brought your coats, because it is going to
be cold. 5 I fear they are cross with me. 6 They did not come
because they were tired. 7 It was impossible for us to go to the
bullfight. 8 You, winning the world cup? *(doubt and mild
derision implied)* 9 Eles vão partir antes de chegarmos. 10 Foi
impossível vermos o ministro. 11 Surpreende-me tu dizeres
uma coisa dessas. *(also: Surpreende-me que tu digas uma . . .)*
12 Disse-lhes adeus antes de partirem. *(also: . . . antes de eles
partirem.)* 13 Não posso dar uma opinião até sabermos tudo.
*(also: . . . até que saibamos tudo. or: enquanto não soubermos
tudo.)* 14 Não tivemos almoço (Não almoçámos) por não
termos tempo. *(also: . . . porque não tivemos tempo.)*

Exercise P.10: sinto-me; escrito; foi; parece; conspirado; tenha; tido; começaram; era; vai; estão; está; sei; chovido; sofreram; deve; causado; lembro; comi; chovido; Estou; pudéssemos; estaríamos; ficariam; Agradeço; irmos; são; creio; vai; aceitámos; fez; passarmos; visitarmos; queremos; possa; forem; podermos; haja; mataria; diga-; conseguirei; dão; prometendo; recordo.

Exercise 31: 1 I have no time to write letters. 2 Mrs Amelia is going to the doctor on Wednesday. 3 My sister is going into hospital on Tuesday for an operation on her throat. 4 I am telling you this for your own good. 5 I haven't hurt you on purpose. (It was inadvertently that I hurt you.) 6 Last month I went to Paris to visit my aunt. 7 Thank you for your kindness. 8 If it is left to me, (Myself/As far as I am concerned/Personally,) I don't mind. 9 Não tenho nenhumas notícias (novidades) para ti. 10 Ele lutou pelos direitos do Homem. 11 Ele foi a Londres em negócios. 12 O senhor vai para casa agora? 13 António foi trabalhar para a Àfrica. 14 Peço desculpa (Desculpe-me) por chegar atrasada/o. 15 Vou para a cama.

Mini-dictionary

Although the following is not an exhaustive list of words found in the book, it will be helpful as a quick reference. Numbers against some entries indicate sections where irregular verbs and other important words are explained. See sections 16, 16a, 18, 19, 20 for days of the week, seasons, numerals and so forth.

a, an um, uma
able capaz; **to be able** poder
abolish abolir
about acerca de; **to be about to** estar para
above acima (de)
abroad estrangeiro, no estrangeiro
accept aceitar
accident acidente
address morada, endereço, direcção; **to address** (someone) dirigir-se a
admire admirar; **to be admired** admirado/a
advertise pôr um anúncio
advertisement anúncio
after depois de
afternoon tarde
against contra
age idade
agree concordar, estar de acordo
all todo/a/s
alone só, sozinho
allow permitir, deixar
almost quase
already já
also também
always sempre
American americano/a

among entre
and e
angry zangado/a; **to be angry/cross** zangar-se com
animal animal
announce anunciar
announcement anúncio
any nenhum/a/s, qualquer, quaisquer
anybody ninguém, qualquer pessoa
anything nada, qualquer coisa
appear aparecer
apple maçã
arrival chegada
arrive chegar
as como, tão
as much/as many tanto/a/s
as soon as assim que
as soon as possible tão depressa **quanto** possível
ask (to enquire) perguntar
ask for pedir
assist ajudar
at *section 10*
at least pelo menos
at once já, imediatamente
attend assistir a
aunt tia
awful terrível, péssimo

243

bad mau, má
badly mal
bank banco
banker banqueiro
bankruptcy falência; to go
bankrupt falir
bath banho
bathtub banheira
bathroom casa sala/quarto de
banho, banheiro (Br)
be ser, estar section 8
beach praia
bear urso
bear (v) aguentar, suportar
beautiful lindo/linda, belo/bela
bed cama, leito
bedroom quarto (de dormir)
beer cerveja
before antes de, perante
begin começar, principiar
behind atrás de
believe crer em, acreditar em
beside ao lado de
besides além de
better melhor
between entre
big grande
bill conta
birthday aniversário; to have a
birthday fazer anos
black preto, negro
blue azul
boat barco
book livro
book (v) marcar, reservar
boring/bored aborrecido sect. 8c
borrow pedir emprestado
both ambos/as; both he and I
tanto eu como ele
bottle garrafa
box caixa, caixote
boy rapaz
bread pão section 22
break (v) quebrar, partir
breakdown (car) avaria; nervous
b. esgotamento nervoso

breakfast pequeno-almoço, café
da manhã (Br)
bring trazer Appendix
brother irmão
brother-in-law cunhado
brown castanho, marron (Br)
brush (n) escova, pincel
bull touro, toiro
bullfight tourada
bus autocarro, ônibus (Br),
machibomba (Mozambique)
business negócio, negócios
but mas
buy comprar
by por section 10, através

call (v) chamar; to be called
chamar-se
can (= to be able) poder
car carro, automóvel
care cuidado; careless
descuidado
carry levar
cat gato/a
certainly certamente, claro, com
certeza
chance oportunidade; by chance
por acaso
change mudança; (v) mudar,
trocar
cheap barato
cheat (v) enganar, fazer batota
cheese queijo
chicken galinha, frango
child/children criança/crianças
choice escolha
choose escolher
Christmas Natal
Christmas Eve Consoada
church igreja
cigarettes cigarros
cigars charutos
citizen cidadão section 22
city cidade
clerk empregado
climb (v) subir, trepar

clock relógio
coach camioneta, carruagem
coat casaco, paletó (*Br*)
coffee café
cold frio
come vir; come in entrar; come back voltar
computer computador
complain queixar-se
complaint queixa
contents conteúdo
continue continuar
cost custo; (*v*) custar
count (*v*) contar
country país; countryside campo
course curso; of course com certeza
cousin primo/a
courage coragem
cover (*v*) cobrir
cross cruz; (*v*) atravessar; to be cross estar zangado, zangar-se
cup chávena, xícara
customer freguês, cliente
customs costumes; alfândega
customs officer funcionário da alfândega

damage prejuízo, dano
dark escuro
darling querido/a
daughter filha
day dia
dead morto
dear caro/a
dentist dentista
die morrer, falecer
diet dieta
difficult difícil
dinner jantar; to dine jantar
dirty sujo
disappear desaparecer
dishonest desonesto/a
disappointed desanimado, desiludido, desapontado
do (*v*) fazer

doctor doutor, médico
door porta
downstairs em baixo, lá/cá em baixo
dream sonho; (*v*) sonhar
dress vestido; to get dressed vestir-se
drink bebida; (*v*) beber
drive conduzir, guiar
drought seca
drunk bêbado, embriagado; to get drunk embriagar-se
dye (*v*) tingír

each cada; each one cada cual; each other um ao outro
ear orelha, ouvido
early cedo
easy fácil; easily facilmente
eat comer
either ou
employment emprego
English inglês
enjoy divertir-se, gozar
enough bastante
enter entrar
equally igualmente
evening tarde, noite, tardinha
every cada
everyday todos os dias
everybody toda a gente, todo o mundo (*Br*)
everything tudo
except excepto
exam exame
examine examinar
example exemplo
exercise exercício
exhibition exposição
expect esperar, contar com
expenses despesas
explain explicar
eye olho

fall (*v*) cair
far longe, distante

farm quinta
fast depressa, adiantado
father pai; **father-in--law** sogro
fault culpa
favour favor
fear medo; (*v*) ter medo, temer, recear
feel (*v*) sentir, sentir-se
fetch buscar, ir buscar
few alguns, poucos
fight (*v*) lutar
fill encher, **fill in** preencher
find achar
finish (*v*) acabar, terminar
fire fogo, incêndio, lume
flat raso; (apartment) andar
flight voo
floor chão, soalho; andar
flower flor
fog nevoeiro
follow seguir
foot pé; **football** futebol
for *sections 10, 48*
foreign estrangeiro
forget esquecer, esquecer-se de
fork garfo
fortnight quinzena, quinze dias
fortunately felizmente
freeze gelar, congelar
French francês
friend amigo/a
from de *section 10*
fruit fruta
full cheio, pleno
furniture mobília; **pieces of furniture** móveis

garden jardim
general geral; (army) general
gentleman cavalheiro, senhor
German alemão *section 22*
get obter, arranjar
get up levantar-se
girl rapariga, moça
give dar
glass vidro, copo, taça

go ir, ir-se embora
go out sair
gold ouro/oiro
good bom/boa; **goodness** bondade
good-bye adeus
goods mercadoria, géneros
grapes uvas
great grande
green verde
grey cinzento
grow crescer
guess (*v*) advinhar
guests convidados

hair cabelo
half metade, meio
hand mâo *section 22*
happen acontecer
happy feliz
hardly mal
hat chapéu
have ter *section 4*
hazard azar
head cabeça
health saúde; **healthy** saudável
hear ouvir
heavy pesado
height altura
help ajuda, socorro; (*v*) ajudar; **help yourself** sirva-se
here aqui, cá
high alto
holidays férias
home casa, lar
hope esperança; (*v*) esperar
horse cavalo
hot quente, calor
hotel hotel
hour hora
house casa
how como *section 13*
however contudo
hunger fome
hurry pressa
hurt (*v*) magoar, ferir

husband marido, esposo

if se
ill doente
immediately imediatamente
important importante
impossible impossível
in em *section 10*
increase aumento; (*v*) aumentar
information informação
intend tencionar
introduce apresentar
invitation convite (*m*)
invite convidar
Italian italiano

Japan Japão; Japanese japonês/a
job emprego, trabalho
journey viagem
juice sumo, suco (*Br*)

keep (*v*) guardar, manter
key chave
kind amável; kindness
  amabilidade
king rei; kingdom reinado
knife faca
know conhecer, saber
knowledge sabedoria,
  conhecimento

lady senhora
lamp candieiro, lâmpada
large grande
last último
late tarde, atrasado
laugh (*v*) rir; laughter riso
law lei, Direito
lawyer advogado
lazy mandrião, preguicoso
learn aprender
leave (*v*) partir, sair; (let go)
  deixar
lemon limão
lend emprestar
less menos

lesson lição
let (*v*) alugar; (allow) deixar
letter carta
lie mentira; to tell a lie mentir
lie down deitar-se
lift elevador; (*v*) levantar, elevar;
  (in car) boleia, carona (*Br*)
light luz; (*v*) acender; (colour)
  claro
like como, semelhante; (*v*) gostar
  de
Lisbon Lisboa
listen ouvir, escutar
little pequeno, pouco
live (*v*) viver; to live at morar
loan empréstimo
London Londres
long longo, comprido
long for (*v*) ter saudades de
longing saudade/s
look (*v*) olhar; look for procurar,
  buscar (*Br*)
lose perder
loss prejuízo, perda
loud alto
love (*v*) amar, gostar de
love (*n*) amor
low baixo
luck sorte; bad luck azar, má
  sorte
lunch almoço
luggage malas, bagagem
lukewarm morno

magazine revista
mail correio; (*v*) pôr no correio
majority maioria, maioridade
make (*v*) fazer; made feito
man homem
mankind homem, os homens, o
  ser humano, humanidade
manager gerente
many muitos
market mercado, praça
married casado; to get married
  casar-se

me/mine *section 28*
meat carne
meet encontrar, encontrar-se com
meeting encontro, reunião
memories memórias,
    recordações
message recado, mensagem
milk leite
mind cérebro, mente; (*v*)
    importar-se *Idiomatic*
    expressions
miss (the train etc) perder;
    (someone/thing) ter
    saudade(s) de
mistake erro; to be mistaken
    estar enganado *section 8c*
money dinheiro
month mês
more mais
moreover além disso, tanto mais
    que
morning manhã
most mais, a maior parte de,
    máximo
mother mãe
mother-in-law sogra
move (*v*) mover, transportar,
    mexer-se, comover; move
    house mudar-se
much muito
music música
must dever
my *section 28*

naked nú/a
name nome
near perto de
nearly quáse
necessary preciso, necessário
need (*v*) precisar de
neighbour vizinho
neither nem
nephew sobrinho
never nunca, jamais
new novo
news notícias, novidades

newspapers jornais
next próximo, a seguir
nice simpático
niece sobrinha
night noite
no, not não
nobody ninguém
noise barulho
nor nem
nothing nada
notice aviso, comunicado; (*v*)
    notar
now agora
number número

obey obedecer
of de *section 10*
office escritório
officer funcionário; (police)
    polícia
often muitas vezes,
    frequentemente
on em *section 10*
once uma vez; at once já,
    imediatamente
only só, somente, apenas
open (*v*) abrir
operation operação
opinion opinião
opportunity oportunidade
or ou
orange laranja
order encomenda; (*v*)
    encomendar, mandar, mandar
    vir
other outro/a; otherwise senão
ought dever
our, ours nosso *section 15*
out fora
owe dever

page página
painter pintor
paper papel
parcel embrulho, pacote
park parque

part parte
partner sócio, parceiro
pay (*v*) pagar
pear pera
peas ervilhas
pen caneta
pencil lápis
people gente, pessoas
pepper pimenta
perhaps talvez
permit autorização, licença
person pessoa
photograph fotografia
pick up (*v*) apanhar
picture quadro, gravura
pin alfinete
pink cor-de-rosa
pipe cano, (*smoking*) cachimbo
pity pena, lástima
plane avião
plate prato
play (*v*) brincar, jogar, tocar
    section 25
pleasant agradável
please por favor, faz favor, faça o
    favor; (*v*) agradar
pleasure prazer, gosto
pocket algibeira, bolso
police polícia
poor pobre
Portuguese português/a
possible possível
post correio; postman carteiro
pound (money) libra
poverty pobreza
prefer preferir
present presente
prevent evitar, impedir
price preço
print (*v*) imprimir
promise prometer
proof prova
protest (*v*) protestar
prove provar
pupil aluno, estudante
purchase compra, compras

purple roxo
put (*v*) pôr; put in meter

quarter quarto
queen rainha
question pergunta, questão
quickly depressa
quiet calado

rabbit coelho
race corrida
railways caminhos de ferro,
    carris
rain chuva: (*v*) chover
rare raro; (steak) mal passado
raw cru, verde
read ler
ready pronto
receive receber
recommend recomendar
red encarnado
refuse (*v*) recusar, recusar-se
regards cumprimentos
remain ficar, continuar
remember lembrar-se de
repeat (*v*) repetir
reply resposta; (*v*) responder
resolve (*v*) resolver, decidir-se a
respect (*v*) respeitar
rest resto, descanso; (*v*)
    descansar
result resultado
resume recomeçar, retomar
return (*v*) voltar, regressar
retire reformar-se, aposentar-se;
    afastar-se
rich rico; richness riqueza
right (-hand) direito; (correct)
    certo; to be right ter razão
ring (*v*) tocar, telefonar
river rio
room quarto, sala, casa
run (*v*) correr

sad triste
safe cofre; to be safe seguro,
    salvo, livre

salary ordenado, salário
salt sal
same mesmo
sample amostra
satisfy satisfazer
say dizer
scarcely apenas, mal
schedule (on) a tempo, à tabela
school escola
scruples escrúpulos
sea mar
season estação
seat lugar, assento
secret segredo
secretary secretária
see ver
seem parecer
send mandar, enviar
serious sério, grave
servant criada, empregada
several vários
shame vergonha
sheet lençol
ship barco, navio
shoe sapato
shop loja
short curto; in short em suma;
    shortly em breve
shortage falta
show espectáculo; (v) mostrar
shut (v) fechar, encerrar
silly tonto, parvo
silver prata
sing cantar
sir senhor
sister irmã
sit down sentar-se
sitting-room sala de estar/de
    visitas
situation situação
skirt saia
sleep (v) dormir; to be sleepy ter
    sono
slow lento, devagar
slowly devagar, lentamente
small pequeno

smell cheiro, aroma
smile (v) sorrir
smoke (v) fumar
so assim, portanto; tão
some algum section 30
something alguma coisa
sometimes às vezes
son filho; son-in-law genho
soon em breve; as soon as assim
    que, logo que
sorry desculpe; to be sorry ter
    pena, pedir desculpa
Spain Espanha; Spanish
    espanhol/a
speak falar
spend gastar
spoon colher
stamp selo
start (v) começar, principiar
station estação
stay (v) ficar
still ainda
story história, conto
street rua
strength força
strike greve
strong forte
study estudo (v) estudar
sugar açúcar
suit fato, terno (Br)
suitcase mala
sun/sunshine sol
supply (v) fornecer
sure (to be) ter a certeza
swim (v) nadar
swimming-pool piscina

table mesa
take tomar, levar, tirar
tall alto
tea chá
teach ensinar
teacher professor/a
tell dizer, contar
telephone telefone
    t. call telefonema, chamada

television televisão
than que, do que
thank (v) agradecer; **thank you**
  obrigado/a
that sections 13, 14
the section 2
theatre teatro
then então
there ali, acolá, lá, aí
there is/are há
therefore portanto
these, this, those section 14
thing coisa
think pensar, crer, achar
thirst sede
throat garganta
throw (v) atirar
thunder trovoada
thus assim
ticket bilhete
time tempo, vez, vagar
tired cansado
to a, para section 10
today hoje section 18
together juntos/as
too também
too much demasiado, de mais
tool ferramenta
touch (v) tocar, apalpar, mexer
  em
town cidadc
train comboio, trem (Br)
travel (v) viajar
traveller viajante
trip volta, giro, pequena
  excursão viagem;
  (v) tropeçar
true verdade, verdadeiro
truth verdade
try tentar, provar, experimentar
turn (v) voltar, virar

ugly feio
umbrella guarda-chuva,
  sombrinha, pára-sol
uncle tio

understand perceber,
  compreender, entender
understanding compreensão,
  entendimento
underneath debaixo de, sob,
  debaixo
unfortunately infelizmente
until até
upstairs em cima, lá em cima
useful útil

very muito
village aldeia, povoação
visit visita; (v) visitar
visa visto
voyage viagem

wait (v) esperar
waiting espera, à espera,
  esperando
waiter criado (de mesa)
walk (v) andar a pé, caminhar,
  passear; (n) passeio
want (v) querer, desejar
warm quente, calor
wash (v) lavar, (oneself) lavar-se
watch relógio; (v) vigiar
water água
way caminho
we/us etc sections 8c, 28
weak fraco
weather tempo
week semana
well (adv) bem; (n) poço
what/when/where/which section
  13
whether se
white branco; whitewash cal
who/whose/whom section 13
whole todo, inteiro
why porque, porquê
wife esposa, mulher
win (v) ganhar
wind vento; windy ventoso
window janela
wine vinho

winter inverno
wish desejo; (*v*) desejar
with com
without sem
woman mulher
word palavra
work trabalho; (*v*) trabalhar
workman operário, trabalhador
world mundo
worried preocupado,
   apoquentado, inquietado,
   aflito
worry (*v*) preocupar-se,
   apoquentar-se
worse pior
worth valor; **to be worth** ter o
   valor de, ser digno de

wound ferida; (*v*) ferir
write escrever
writer escritor/a
written escrito

year ano
yearly anual, por ano,
   anualmente
yellow amarelo
yes sim
yesterday ontem *section 18*
yet ainda, no entanto, contudo
you/yours etc *sections 7, 15*
young jovem
youth juventude

Index

The numbers refer to section headings, *not* pages.

Picture Credits

Jacket: All special photography Paul Harris, Clive Streeter,
Linda Whitwam.